A HUNDRED LAST BREATHS

A Hundred Last Breaths is one of the most impactful pieces I have ever read.... It's a validation for everyone who's ever been a [cancer] caregiver, and it can serve to provide support for those in a similar position.

—Allsion Owen Smith

Raw and riveting and beautifully written.

—Beth Leas

The vulnerability, raw, real, and so human-ness of this memoir left me in awe. Publishing this work is an offering to humanity and an incredible example of post-traumatic growth.

—Donna Vella

Bardolf & Company

A HUNDRED LAST BREATHS
Caregiving at the End of Life with Acceptance, Compassion, and Love

ISBN 978-1-938842-80-1
Copyright © 2025 by Matthew Broad

Bardolf & Company
www.bardolfandcompany.com

Cover art by Lena Robinson Art
Instagram: *lenarobinsonart*

Mandala art by Matthew Broad
Instagram: *mateofreehandmandala*
www.freehandmandala.com

I dedicate this book
to Janet,
my beloved partner,
who gave me the gift
of allowing me to assist her
in life and death.

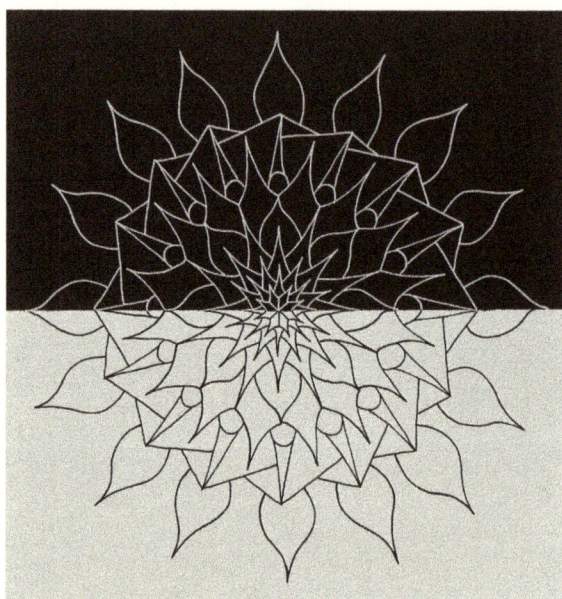

A HUNDRED LAST BREATHS

Caregiving at the End of Life with Acceptance, Compassion, and Love

Matthew Broad

Bardolf & Company
Sarasota, Florida

Foreword

Grief is never a single moment. It is a continuum—a slow unfolding that begins long before a final breath is taken. In the time leading up to Janet's passing, Matthew was living within what we, in the field of counseling, call *anticipatory grief*. This is the kind of grief that begins when we realize that loss is coming, even as we continue to love, hope, and care for a loved one.

In *A Hundred Last Breaths*, Matthew opens a window into this space between life and loss. Over the course of nine months, he recorded his days as Janet's primary caregiver, her companion and witness. Through his words, we see both the beauty and the burden of loving someone through a difficult journey with cancer. What emerges is not only the story of Janet's final chapter, but also a tribute to their shared life—the courage, exhaustion, and tenderness that defined their time together.

I first met Matthew one week after Janet's passing, when he contacted Ann's Place for grief counseling. From the beginning, it was clear that the love he carried for Janet was vast and unwavering. It was also clear that his grief had depth - not just sorrow, but a kind of sacred responsibility to remember, to honor, and to give meaning to the years they shared. As our sessions unfolded, Matthew often spoke not only of loss, but of caregiving. From small joys to the ache of watching someone you love, dramatically change. In those conversations, and later through his writing, I recognized the familiar emotional rollercoaster I have witnessed in many caregivers.

As someone who has facilitated caregiver support groups for several years, I know how often caregivers' voices go unheard.

Their stories are full of resilience, yet rarely do we see them told with such honesty. This book offers what so many need but struggle to articulate: validation. It tells the truth about what it means to care for someone who is dying.

Matthew's journal entries are intimate and unfiltered. He does not write from hindsight or with sound conclusions. Instead, he invites us into the rawness of each day—his shifting of emotions, the quiet acts of care and the courage to keep showing up for Janet. His transparency is the book's greatest gift. It reminds readers that there is no single "right" way to love.

As an art therapist, I often see grief expressed not in words but in color, form, and texture. I see how people create what feels unspeakable into something tangible. Matthew has done this with language. His writing is its own kind of art. It is an emotional landscape painted in real time. Through his journal entries, he captures the movement of caregiving and the complexity of anticipatory grief, offering readers a safe space to feel their feelings.

A Hundred Last Breaths is, above all, an act of love. It honors Janet—her life, her energy, and the spiritual partnership she and Matthew built. But it also honors the caregivers who will see themselves reflected in these pages. Matthew's willingness to share this journey reminds us that caregiving is not a single role, but a profound expression of humanity. It is both a privilege and a heartbreak. And while grief may transform over time, the kind of love that fills these pages, remains constant.

I am deeply grateful for Matthew's courage in bringing his story forward. May this book offer validation to those who have walked the caregiver's path, and understanding to those who wish to know what love looks like at its most selfless.

— Debbie Mendez, ATR, LPC-A
Counselor and Art Therapist, Ann's Place

Introduction

This is not only a story but an actual day-by-day journal of my experience of taking care of my beloved life partner, Janet, and all that we went through together on her cancer journey.

It started as "the morning pages," an attempt to write every morning with my cup of coffee, before I got on with the day. The idea behind writing every morning was to help with a bit of a "block" I was having in regard to the creative process for my artwork—painting mandalas. But instead of what I intended it to do with my painting, it provided me a sense of release and a form of therapy as the intensity and responsibilities of caring for my beloved Janet got harder. It quickly turned into a daily journal.

I realized as I was writing how difficult it was to articulate what I was feeling and experiencing, and I questioned why I was doing it many times. But I pushed through and tried to write every day regardless of whether I felt good or bad, tired or pissed off, loved or lonely. It became therapeutic for me in so many ways.

Writing gave me a sense of being able to articulate how I was feeling as the process of Janet's decline unfolded. Writing helped me reflect on what was happening not only to Janet but to me and my relationship with her and to our experience with the dying process.

When I was going through this experience, some close friends and family members kept suggesting that I should eventually write a book about it. For a while, I thought I might call it *The Roller Coaster Ride*. But as I sat in the waiting room of the cancer treatment hospital, the last time I took Janet in for treatment, I realized that life, from the moment we are born to the time we pass on to whatever comes next, is a roller coaster ride of emotions, experiences, ups and downs, and trials and tribulations—good moments and bad moments, feelings of sadness and feelings of joy. We are all on a roller coaster ride, whether we want to be or not; it is the human condition.

Then, during the last seven weeks of hospice care for Janet, I felt like I was watching her last breath hundreds of times...and so here is *A Hundred Last Breaths*.

* * *

A week after Janet passed, I sat down and read my entire journal. Although it was emotional. As I read it, it took me right back to each and every moment, and I felt them all over again. I felt overwhelmed. It was difficult to understand what I and we had just gone through. All of the questioning I was doing: questioning my faith and beliefs, why this was happening to Janet, and how to be the best caregiver I could be. I realized that by allowing myself to be vulnerable and making my journal public, other people who are going through loss, grief, and the sometimes long and difficult road of caregiving may find some solace in knowing they are not alone. That other people feel these feelings and questions as well. I realized that what I had written could help others who are going through caring for a loved one with a terminal illness.

So, here it goes: It is my truth. What I witnessed, and how I felt. I continue to learn more about myself with every breath I take.

Acceptance, Compassion, and Love.

* * *

Fair warning: I imagine that some topics I touch on might be "triggering" to a reader. If this is the case and you feel you need help, please refer to the end of the book where I have listed some organizations that can offer support.

In Gratitude

I have endless and special gratitude for the following people in our lives, without whose support and love, I could not have made it through these past seven years. I'm sure they have their own stories about their journey regarding their relationship with Janet during this difficult period. Janet was a light that shone bright for all of us and will continue to as we remember the times we like to remember and the times we don't.

Marlon, Karen, Karl, Lena, Michael, Kaelan, Aja, Dagan, Lois, Ken, Dana, and the hundreds of people we knew and didn't know who donated to our many fundraisers over the years. You are all a blessing to me and my family.

As a reference for you, the reader, I have included a list of people in order of appearance whom I refer to and how they are related to me or Janet.

IT REALLY DOES TAKE A VILLAGE

Many people and organizations helped care for Janet and me by visiting, spending time, and offfering their assistance. Rather than take the time to explain who they were in the journal entries, I have listed them here, to keep the narrative flow as close to the original writing as possible.

1. **Dana** shared in the responsibilities of running the Yoga Loft Studio with Janet. Her compassion, love, and unwavering support were essential for us to care for Janet the way we did.

2. **MSK** is Memorial Sloan Kettering Cancer Center in NYC and Harrison, New York, where Janet received most of her treatments.

3. **Chris** is Janet and my friend and an Acupuncturist.

4. **Jen** is Janet's and my friend who had four dear friends who passed away from cancer in a short amount of time.

5. **Kaelan** is my son who lives in Brooklyn.

6. **Tim** is Janet's Nephew.

7. **Marlon** is Janet's 23-year-old.

8. **Karen** is Janet's sister from Atlanta, who I consider an Angel in human form.

9. **Lena** is my sister who lives in Florida.

10. **Michael** is Lena's husband, my brother-in-law, who lives in Florida.

11. **Lois** is Janet's mother, who lives in Essex, Connecticut.

12. **Dagan** is my son who lives in Vermont.

13. **Aja** is my son who lives in Atlanta.

14. **Natasha** is Janet's friend from a previous working relationship.

15. **Remony** is my and Janet's friend from high school.

16. **Phyllida** is Janet's and my friend from high school and is Remony's sister.

17. **Kenny** is Janet's friend from college.

18. **Andrew** is my brother who passed away a year before.

19. **TLC** is a local networking group that I am connected to.

20. **Beth** is the owner and coordinator of TLC.

21. **Ken** is Janet's stepfather, married to Lois.

22. **Karl** is Karen's husband and Janet's brother-in-law.

23. **Suzy** is Janet's friend from the yoga studio.

24. **Nancy** is Janet's lifelong friend from her childhood neighborhood.

25. **Taylor** is Janet's friend from the yoga studio and is married to Chris.

26. **Gretchen** is Janet's lifelong friend from her childhood neighborhood.

27. **Allison** is Janet's high school friend.

28. **Margaret** is Janet's high school friend.

29. *Phish* is my and Dagan's favorite band.

30. **Maid** is Medical Assistance In Death, an organization in Vermont designed to help people with terminal illness transition with dignity.

31. **Chrissy** is the social services representative with The Proton Radiation Center in New York City.

32. **Sonic Ice** is the ice Janet discovered at Hope Lodge in NYC that you can only get at Sonic Restaurants.

33. **Natalie** is Janet's and my friend from high school, and a reflexologist extraordinaire.

34. **Phillipe** and **David** are my friends who came to drum bedside with me.

35. **Elliot** is my friend who lives in Vermont.

36. **Moo** is a stuffed Highland Cow that Marlon gave to Janet when she came home for hospice.

37. **Kimberly** is Janet's stepsister.

38. **Leslie**, **Greg**, and daughter **Gulia** are Janet's and my friends.

39. **Lars** is my and Janet's friend.

40. **Ann's Place** is a cancer support center in Danbury, Connecticut.

41. **Willa** is Janet's friend and co-worker at the yoga studio.

42. **Debbie** is my grief therapist from Ann's Place

43. **Jenny** is Janet's co-worker at the yoga studio.

44. **Giovanna** is my and Janet's friend and Lena's lifelong best friend.

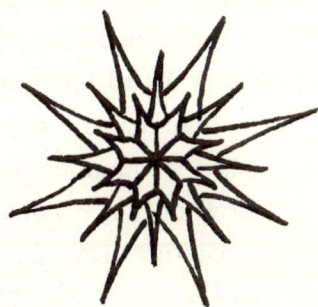

Beginnings

I was born in the UK and raised in Connecticut. After my mom tried to commit suicide when I was fifteen, we moved, and I went to a high school in Cross River, New York. That is where Janet and I met. We had many mutual friends as we travelled in similar circles. Janet was on the tennis team, and I was on the baseball team. Both our friend groups outside of sports were hippies playing Ultimate frisbee in bare feet and loving the music of the Grateful Dead and Neil Young. We all loved and spent time in nature at the local Ward Pound Ridge Reservation and attended many parties together. Although we were never more than "just friends," when we reunited almost thirty years later, I always claimed that we did have one kiss in high school, but Janet said that was only in my dreams.

I was a rebellious teenager and barely graduated from high school. Then, I spent three years learning how to be a carpenter before everyone convinced me to go to college for construction engineering at a SUNY (State University of New York) school in Canton. There, I met my future and eventually ex-wife. We got married after and traveled around the country following the Grateful Dead, making a living selling tie-dye clothing. Neither of us wanted to do the traditional 9-to-5 career thing.

Then, we landed in Brattleboro, Vermont. Brattleboro was an amazing community at that time, and we felt like we could settle down there. We were there for 23 years. Throughout the roller coaster of life and all the ups and downs, I always felt the extremes of the responsibilities of being married, having a family, and what it takes to support a family of five being a carpenter and the sole breadwinner.

In 1994, there was a recession in the Northeast, and I had to figure out how to earn a living without building houses. I created a small business of making hand drum instruments to sell to music stores. Surprisingly, it took off, so much so that I had to hire help and again had more responsibilities with many employees. In the early 2000s, I became so overwhelmed that I had a midlife crisis. I felt I was being crushed by the responsibilities of taking care of everyone else but myself. Getting into therapy and anti-depressants made life bearable. I "soldiered through" and had many joyful moments with my kids living in Vermont.

In 2009, when my marriage of 23 years was falling apart, I met Janet at a high school reunion, and we fell deeply in love. Once we were both divorced from our respective spouses, we moved in together. We both felt that we saved each other's lives.

In 2014, I became a property manager of an estate in Connecticut, which enabled me to have some time to pursue teaching hand drumming, making pies, gardening, and creating art by painting mandalas. I have realized through this writing process that I have always been creative; always worked with my hands to build houses, make drums, paint, and teach. All things that I credit to being a part of my family history, as both of my parents were artists and creators of beautiful things, from paintings to quilts, from writing to baking cakes. During this time, Janet was transitioning from being an administrator at a private middle school to being trained as a yoga instructor. That process led to her becoming the full-time director of a yoga studio in Bedford, New York, called The Yoga Loft

Our living situation made it possible for me to be able to take care of Janet the way I did, but I didn't start writing until the beginning of Janet's decline into stage IV cancer in the fall of 2024, and I continue to write each day ever since.

Sept 2024 entry

Five years ago this week, we found out that Janet had colon cancer. That is when this extremely challenging journey began. Challenging in ways that I had no idea what or how I would get through it all. Am I really capable of unconditional love? Love without conditions? Being a caregiver for someone with stage IV cancer is when unconditional love is necessary. The "conditions" would be to fully accept her choices, no matter how those choices would be affecting me and my physical and emotional well-being, because SHE has the cancer. It has been a full-on roller-coaster ride from the beginning, where on the good days, I have fully accepted everything that goes along with her choices. The choice of going through 59 rounds of chemo treatments, and on the bad days, feeling like I can't go on another day. There have been times when I have felt more alone than I have ever felt in my entire life, both physically and emotionally. The complications of a relationship with yourself and with your partner when the struggle to survive is based around multiple surgeries and many rounds of poison.

A year before the cancer diagnosis, Janet had a femoral nerve sheath tumor removed from her left femoral nerve. The surgery could have resulted in her being unable to feel her left leg. Leading up to surgery, every night I would put a layer of ice on the bed for her to lie on and then cover her abdomen with ice just to give her a little relief from the nerve pain. I am happy to say the surgery was a success. It took her six weeks to recover before she went back to work at the Yoga Loft in Bedford, New York, where she is co-director with Dana, as well as a yoga instructor.

In October of 2019, she had surgery to remove part of her colon and the cancer tumor. Stage III colon cancer, which was found in a routine colonoscopy. After four weeks of recovery, she returned to work at the Yoga Loft and started 12 rounds of chemo every other week. In the first round, Janet almost died from her body going into shock from the concoction that the oncologist prescribed.

It took three rounds for the oncologist to find the right potency that her body could handle. The routine would be to sit in the chair at the treatment center for four+ hours, go home with a slow-release chemo bag attached to her port, and throw up for a few days. The bag would be detached two days later. It would take about five days for her to "rebound" enough to have the energy to go back to work. Seven days later, she would do it all over again. This went on for six months, when the next scan showed that no cancer could be found. Woohoo! What a relief.

This all happened as the world was shutting down because of Covid. Although everyone was masking and keeping their distance from everyone else, concerned they'd catch it, we had already gone through six months of it because we didn't want any additional sickness for Janet while she was undergoing chemo.

To the extent that we all ended up experiencing masking and social distancing as a collective, it was an amazing time for us. We were relieved that the cancer wasn't present and focused on gardening, when we got an amazing opportunity to take care of a farm garden in Bedford. Janet also worked with the owners of the Yoga Loft to create an outdoor patio that could be used for ongoing yoga classes while Covid was spreading around the world.

Then, in August of 2022, a scan showed that the cancer had metastasized to her liver and peritoneal cavity. This news was devastating for all of us. We had had such a great year being together, creating and doing the things we loved.

Janet made the move to an MSK (Memorial Sloan Kettering) oncologist, and, after lengthy discussion, it was decided that she would have surgery to remove the part of the liver where the tumors were and, at the same time, remove the tumor in the peritoneal cavity. During the six-hour surgery in New York, when they opened her up, they found the tumors were lodged right up against her uterus, so they gave her a full hysterectomy. This came as quite a shock after the fact, and it took some time for Janet to come to terms with this. After five weeks of recovery, she went back to work at the Yoga Loft. She also started another 12 rounds of a different chemo concoction and another routine that went like this: treatment > vomiting > pain > vomiting > rebound.

Near the end of the summer of 2023, a scan showed that the tumors had regrown in Janet's liver. Her oncologist and liver doctor felt the only option left would be to install a hepatic pump in her abdomen, a device with a catheter that would deliver chemo via an artery directly to the liver, rather than systemically through the port in her chest. He told us that Janet was a "perfect" candidate for this procedure. The plan was to pump 400 times stronger chemo than before. During the surgery to install the pump, which happened in September of 2023, the doctors also cut out more of Janet's liver.

Because this surgery not only removed things from her body, but also put things in, Janet recovered more slowly than before. It took her two months before she went back to work. The doctors wanted to make sure she was strong enough for the more powerful treatment, so they didn't start putting the chemo in the pump until mid-December. To everyone's surprise, Janet didn't have any side effects at all—no aches and pain, no throwing up, no mouth sores, no hair loss. She was able to go back to work the day after treatment. Life began to feel "normal" for her and for me. The routine of work, eating, and limited exercise allowed Janet to look into alternative healing modalities as well. We knew that acupuncture and massage therapies were a mainstay in helping with stress and body aches successfully.

In the middle of March 2024, Janet went to see someone who used a technique called "cupping" on both sides and up and down her spine. The method goes back more than 3,000 years in China and ancient Egypt. Practitioners use special cups to create suction that pulls at the skin and underlying tissue, improving blood flow and promoting healing. It's typically done on the back and shoulders and employed for athletes to reduce pain or stress in the muscles.

Unbeknownst to Janet and the cupping therapist, the technique pulled the 400-times-stronger chemo out of her liver and into the rest of her body. A couple of days later, her body began to shut down from the toxicity, and her organs and mind went into shock. Janet had what I call a near-death experience. She was experiencing so much pain she thought she was having a heart attack, and when I looked into her eyes, I couldn't see Janet's life force, just big black pupils. I was terrified and was about to call 911 when she got some words out... she said, "Call Chris." Fortunately, Chris, a dear friend and acupuncturist, happened to be home when I called him at 10 pm. He came right over, and the two of us managed to get Janet to calm her breathing. We massaged her with calming oils, and Chris did some acupuncture. He stayed with us long into the night, and we got her through it. I put a call into the oncologist whose assistant recommended that I take Janet to the closest emergency room at Stamford Hospital, where she ended up on their cancer care floor. The doctors there couldn't understand why she was in such a condition and couldn't do anything for her except give her Tylenol for the pain and keep her hydrated.

After a few days, I brought Janet home. But the pain and extreme discomfort continued, and she curled up into a fetal position, unable to move. I ended up bringing her to the MSK emergency room in New York for what ended up being three weeks of testing. Because no one really understood what cupping does, the doctors couldn't determine what it was that caused Janet to have this harrowing experience. The doctors on the colon cancer recovery floor thought that the time had come to prepare for her demise. It was truly terrifying for both of us.

Janet tolerated the tests as much as she could, but after three weeks of poking and prodding and with very little sleep, she decided it was time to go home. After all, a hospital room is not the place for resting with all the equipment beeping, nurses waking you up every three hours to take your vitals, and the families of roommates coming and going and talking on their phones. So I brought Janet home, and in the quiet of our house and with nourishing food, she began to come back to life.

After two weeks, she was able to walk every day. For two months, Janet rested, ate well, and took in the most beautiful spring we had experienced in the 16 years we had been together by enjoying nature on our walks. During the testing, the doctors had found that the tumors in her liver had grown and that there was a blood clot pressing against one of them, so I had to give her a blood thinner shot two times a day in her belly. I did this for four months; it was really hard for both of us.

Janet went back to work in June. She and her oncologist wanted to give her liver a rest and decided to wait before resuming treatments. The oncologist also thought that the pump wasn't working and that Janet should start back up with systemic chemo at the end of July. Janet agreed and went back on the original Oxolyplatin/Arinotican concoction from five years earlier. Unfortunately, it made her very sick, and she was in extreme pain for three days before she "rebounded." However, she was able to go back to work at the beginning of August.

As of today, Janet has one more treatment before we go on a family trip to Europe. Although her energy picked up for the trip, we all knew that it would probably be the last time we could travel. We were all determined to have this time together while Janet still could.

Janet will get new scans when we get back to determine the next phase, whatever that may be.

Day 1
November 10, 2024

Is there really a connection with the divine that can be consciously attained, or will the mystery always be a mystery? What can I possibly say to our friend Jen after hearing that four of her friends died within two weeks and knowing that death, grief, and what is coming for Janet? Janet's skin itches her all the time, and it seems to be deteriorating in a way. I am noticing the changes in her body and her mind slowing down…. The changes in my body as well as I age, now that I am on a medicine to help me feel the sensation of urinating. I don't like it. Sometimes I feel that I don't want to live in this world anymore. I wish I could be more positive for myself and others, to be excited about life. To be able to apply the "nuggets" of meaning and morals from the movies I watch and the stories I hear, to be a better person.

The agents of chaos seem to be getting stronger, and innocent people are being negatively affected. I find it's such a struggle to come to terms with the ways of the world right now. Sometimes I feel that humans are the cancer on the planet. Is cancer created from fear? What is fear, and why do we experience it? Fear of death, her death, their death, my death…from the collective trauma of pain, loneliness. Be productive, have a purpose, make money, don't be depressed about life's responsibilities, and the "lack" of happiness.

I've always believed the flow of energy in > energy out, and in and out. Making love is an in-and-out movement sometimes. No one will read this, it's ok to say it…I am lonely for sex and love making…the grief rises coming from not having the relationship with Janet as it was before the cancer. Did I think that it was not going to change things... like everything? Of course, everything changes, I know change to be the one constant. Change.

Day 2
November 11, 2024

Old age is weird. I'm 62. Some would say that's not old. But it feels old to me at the moment. It's hard not to feel my body declining. Of course, not in the same way Janet's is declining from the cancer, but I am feeling slower, achier, and more reflective about time and life in general. I think about my mom and dad a lot, and their last few years. Where were they when they were my age, and what were they doing in relation to what their kids were doing? Maybe I should call these daily writings "What would Matthew do?" If I am looking for guidance from the Source or God, which I believe is in me....

Janet is trying hard to survive, although I sometimes wonder why, with the deterioration that she is going through. I notice and don't say anything because...what's the point? It would only cause worry for her. I have accepted the demise of our bodies, hers, mine, people's around me, but it doesn't make the grief any easier. I'm already experiencing the loneliness of not having what we had in our relationship, everything from lovingly holding hands to being spontaneous, having deep conversations, intimacy on all levels, fun, and enjoyment of wanting to be with each other... it's all gone.

We are five years and two months since her cancer diagnosis. If it were me, according to the doctors, I'd be dead by now because I wouldn't have gone the chemo route. Maybe the question for Matthew is: Why can't I be positive for all the waking moments of my life? Answer: Because of the programming and traumatic experiences that have negatively impacted the cells of my brain and body. They want to hold on to the trauma as a defense, to justify the "not worthy" of feeling good, especially when others around me are not feeling good. And there is injustice, pain, and death in the world. The question might look like this instead: How can I be positive all the time? Answer: Your soul is positive all the time. Tapping into that is your work in this present body and mind. Another day will come and go so fast because that is what is happening. The concept of time is changing for so many of us. It's funny how I feel like my body is slowing down, but the sensation of time is speeding up. I wonder if that is because the end for everything is getting closer… the end of everything on this physical plane… "the world as we know it."

Day 3
Nov 12

The caregiver group Zoom meeting brought tears to my eyes today as I shared how intense it was when Janet almost passed in the spring. I tried to relate how important it is to look after yourself as a caregiver and that it is ok to express your emotions when you are going through the shit, even though you feel you have to be the pillar of strength for the person you are caring for. Feeling overwhelmed totally sucks, and that is when the depression can set in and stay for a while.

As I heard the other stories, I realized that maybe my situation wasn't as bad as theirs. I guess after five years, we have settled into a sense of acceptance and "one-day-at-a-time" approach, dealing with issues as they come. Like the full-body rash that came out of nowhere yesterday, or the allergic reaction from the cupping last spring, which almost killed her. We were able to rebound. Now the tumors have clumped together to make one big growth in her liver. So we have a new plan: Direct Proton Radiation every day for 15 consecutive days. So, I wasn't so happy to hear someone in the Zoom meeting say that her father passed away from the radiation.

I spent some time with Kaelan the other day. I love hanging out with my kids. It's definitely my happy place, doing the things we all love doing together, going to movies, watching TV, going to concerts. It's so great that we all love doing these things.

Day 4
Nov 13

Terrible night for Janet, itching and suffering. She took a Benadryl and a 5mg THC gummy and finally went back to sleep around 3 a.m. I feel so bad for her. If this doesn't let up soon, she is going to lose her will to be alive. Janet said a couple of times yesterday, "I hope this isn't it", and "I welcome the end just to get me out of this body." When she says shit like that, it makes me feel that, yes, this really could be "it" for her. The full-body rash is the worst I have ever seen, worse than Dad's just before he passed. FUCK, FUCK, FUCK!!!

When I walk and think about what the end might look like for Janet and hope the suffering goes away, it is really intense. Holding her warm body, lying next to her while she is itching and suffering and moaning all night.... Sometimes I have to keep checking to see if her body is still warm, and I feel terrified of that moment when her body becomes permanently cold. I know when it happens, there will be some sense of relief as well, that she won't be suffering in this body anymore. How can you possibly prepare for it, for this? I know it's bad when she asks me for gummies in the middle of the night; she's never done that before. So many pills. Her body and liver must be so overtaxed. My theory is that her liver just can't handle it all. And with the 8.5 cm tumor clump.... Fucking sucks big time!

Keep writing! What's the use? If the end is near anyway? Whose end, Janet's end, my end, everyone's end? How can I be a positive force when I have these thoughts and feelings? One day at a time, one moment at a time. Listen to music, go for walks, keep writing, open the mail, take action, get unstuck! Do another video diary.

Why do I keep drinking this morning coffee? Addiction to routine. It's really hard to choose to break the comforting habits of routine and addictions. What is the comfort factor all about? Maybe to give me a sense that everything is all right.
Andrew died, Jack died, Mom died, Dad died. The moving on… Janet will die, I will die. Sometimes I wish I would die already to relieve the mental anguish that swirls in my head every day… almost every day.

The external pressures of living in this material world and paying taxes.… Who the fuck are they to put a tax on things, on me, when there is so little money already.… Fuckers! Janet just woke up and asked for prednisone meds with milk. Hopefully, it will give her some relief. The rash is more down the legs now and less on the chest.

Day 5
Nov 15

Up a bit later today…Coffeeeeee. Janet's rash isn't as intense today. Her back and chest have cleared up, but now it's on her feet. It seems like it's moving through her whole body. What a mystery. Maybe it's some sort of systemic reaction from what they are putting in her hepatic pump. This is day four of the rash. I am really hoping it goes away fully. It is so hard to see her suffering so much over the last few days. She is up and getting ready for work…. Pictures of Janet's rash are being sent to the oncologist team.

Day 6
Nov 16

Rough night for both of us. Janet's rash came back in a few places before she went to bed last night. The doctor says that it is from the liver "cleaning out." The itching is clearly driving her crazy, and it is so hard to watch. I just want her to have some relief and stop itching! At first, I tried to help her physically stop itching, but now I've stopped trying to stop her from itching herself and accept that she can't stop it. Dana thankfully got a sub for Janet at work, so hopefully she can rest. Thank God for Dana. What a perfect business partnership match for Janet these past few years. I am so grateful for her! So many great changes at the Bedford Post with new owners: the trouble child yoga instructor isn't there anymore, and the energy on the property has shifted for the better, which is helping reduce the stress in Janet's life.

Unfortunately, when I look at Janet's face today, I feel that her end is near. Her eyes, her skin, and her overall tone due to the latest setback with the rash. To me, it feels like her body is breaking down. Of course, I would never say that to her, and wonder how she pushes through with her energy and her will to live. I would have given up years ago.

We are supposed to go see *Dark Star Orchestra* in concert tonight at the Capitol Theater. I can't imagine she will have the strength to go and hope she will stay home to rest.

Day 7
Nov 17

The rash on Janet seems to be lessening. We both went to the DSO concert. It was fun—the music, conversation with a friend. Thank you, Michael and Lena, for the birthday gift, allowing Janet and me to go to one last concert together.

Day 8
Nov 18

The coffee is good this morning! Janet went to see Chris yesterday. He says that her liver is struggling to work, and that is why the rash is on her skin, and that he doesn't think the radiation is a good idea and could lead to her liver failing. I wonder what liver failure looks like and what it would mean as far as how sick she would be? Hospitalization? Dying in the hospital? I know that is not what she wants, to be in the hospital again. She goes to talk to the radiologist on Wednesday. It's been almost two months since her last treatment. You would think that the cancer is growing, but Chris says she should hold off, not rush into treatment.

I still manage to walk two miles two times a day, and that feels good. I plan on starting a new painting today. Every day I think about eating a gummy or smoking weed to help put me in a "carefree" state of mind, but then I think: What if Janet's liver fails and I need to make some emergency decisions? I need to have a clear mind and be able to do the right thing… whatever that means?

I must admit that all this life stuff and world bullshit makes me want to escape and "live in the woods" again. I guess that is why I ended up in Vermont for a simpler life back in 1987. It presents a whole bunch of other problems to be solved and struggles to be faced. Probably the same struggles, just in a different setting. Health, money, politics, where to live. It makes you realize the privilege of what you have compared to being homeless, jobless, family-less, friendless.

As I keep writing each day, I attempt to make the thought connection to the hand to be able to write some sort of bullshit that makes sense, or something that is just a bunch of garbage spewing out on the paper… blah, blah, blah. Like the first tie-dye I made back in 1986. It had a mix of orange and green and ended up with a big brown splotch on it. It looked like someone had wiped their ass with it. Someone still bought it! Just proof that "beauty is in the eye of the beholder."

Really, the only thing that isn't beautiful to anyone is pain, struggle, and death, although now that I/we have been through so much pain and struggle, death is looking more and more like a beautiful option every day. What can I say? When you say, "I'll pray," who or what are you praying to? A god? A higher being? Someone or something that can make things better or change things in your favor? Hmmm. What would Matthew think or do? I guess Matthew would just question it all, no clear answer, but maybe to "have faith" that in the END, everything will be ok, whatever ok means. Love and compassion, empathy, and being kind to the best of your ability are really all that can be done. "I'll pray for you" has just become the thing that people want to hear because they have all been brainwashed into thinking that a higher being has the final say and can help with the pain and the struggle and give you some sort of relief: God bless you, bless you, my child, have faith that you will be ok, because death will come and your spirit will move on to something else. Probably blend into the cosmic source… or nothingness.

Day 9
Nov 19

As we sat watching TV last night, I looked over to Janet a few times, wondering how she really feels. She looks tired and worn out, more so each day. She hasn't walked with me in a long time. I think it's because she is too tired. It seems like the cancer is really taking its toll, along with the 59 treatments of chemo and all the drugs she takes daily. The rash has really affected her psychologically, and she wonders if "this is it." I am trying to accept how she is every day, up or down, energetic or tired. I know that she is doing her best to be positive, and I am doing my best to allow her to be whatever she is…from moment to moment.

I had my first individual caregiver therapy session yesterday with a therapist from Memorial Sloan Kettering Cancer Center. They are giving me seven free sessions as part of a study about caregivers' wellbeing. It's a good thing they are free because our funds are pretty bad right now. The once-a-week talk therapy is going to be helpful. I know it is.

At the end of the session, after I gave some backstory and was honest about how I am feeling today, the therapist said that I have done an incredible job these past five years. Because the ups and downs have been so hard, it is difficult for me to think I have done a good job, not only as a caregiver for Janet, but taking care of myself. I wonder about my acceptance of the "terminal" impending, sooner-than-later death for Janet. I have roller-coastered about it so much that I almost feel numb about how I feel. I am not freaking about it, just feel sad and nervous about how to handle her death logistically. Shouldn't I be more worried and maybe even panicked about it? She looks sick all the time to me. Her face is puffy and discolored, her body shape has changed, mostly due to the hepatic pump, and her skin is scarred up all over, not only from the surgeries but also from the recent rash. And before that, the bloody spots that just kept happening for months, which have left tiny bumps all over her. This slow body and mind deterioration really sucks so bad!

There is so much I want to talk to Janet about that I worry will put her more into a state of depression and anxiety. So, I don't do it. Maybe I'll say to her that she needs to tell me when I should seriously prepare for how she wants it to end. Although I'm not sure she will talk about it because she really wants to get to the next milestone of Tim's wedding in June in Seattle. I really am taking it one day at a time. It's the best I can do, and so the long-term plans need to be kept in mind—that what happens could be with or without Janet.

I am still walking the path twice a day, which I love so much because I am seeing the natural cycles of the deer, turkeys, and squirrels, as well as the woodpeckers. When Janet was recovering from her near-death experience in the spring, we watched the property come alive as we walked, so it's great to see it circle back to its dormant winter state. Janet has obviously been too tired to walk with me. It used to really bum me out that I was walking by myself, but again, having gone past the acceptance of being alone has allowed me to enjoy my solo walks. Also, the walking is like a silent meditation with an occasional conversation with Bucky the 8-point deer who watches me pass by.… I have too many pictures of Bucky. It's amazing where my mind goes while I am walking. Fantasizing about life, the what ifs, past, present, and future times. Trying to roll with it and enjoy the ride, as so many philosophers recommend. Yoda would say, "There is no try, there is just do."

Day 10
Nov 20

Janet's rash is almost gone except on her feet, so that's a big relief! That was some terrible suffering.

Day 11
Nov 22

Janet is awake and making her coffee. The last few days have been hard for me to watch her be so tired and sick-looking. Accepting it is the only way, and to love her even when she doesn't want to be held. It's not comfortable holding her because of all the surgeries and the pump and the port and the cancer. Attempting to seems to make her feel unwell. She doesn't want to be touched very much. Even handholding seems to have gotten hard for her, like she has no interest in the smallest affection. The only thing is "spooning" when we sleep, and even that can be uncomfortable.

Acceptance > Compassion > Love...

Day 12
Nov 23

Acceptance > Compassion > Love

Waking up with a foggy mind and blurry eyes, I feel like my dreams are just on the surface of my awake state. As I write this morning, I keep seeing something out of the corner of my eye… It's either a "floater" in my vision (I don't think it is because it doesn't happen all the time) or an energy that I catch a glimpse of—something or someone watching and hanging around in a different reality or dimension. You know, there are so many movies and stories about different worlds, good and bad, infinite possibilities. At the moment, the reality we're in seems to have quite a bit of suffering for me and Janet, and Marlon.

Where are my kids at? At their homes, sleeping as far as I can see. Except for the entertainment of movies and TV shows, I am feeling like I am done with AI technology and computering. I do wish I could feel happy and grateful more of the time or for more moments of it. Maybe it's not just acceptance, compassion, and love of others but of myself that will help ease the struggle, the pain, the sadness, and the grief.

Yesterday, I was scrolling music videos on Instagram and saw one with an incredible dance troupe. Every dancer was doing the same choreographed moves. The second time I watched it, I broke down sobbing. The feelings of such beauty and amazement, along with sadness and grief, came to the surface of my being. It lasted for maybe two minutes and then, like a light switch, it stopped. It just goes to show you that I have emotions that can get triggered in an instant by being exposed to beautiful art. Always close to the surface, ready to bubble out for a sense of relief.

Sometimes I wonder, when Janet passes, how much emotion will surface? Will I become numb and not be able to cry, or will I cry hard and long, or will it come and go? With all this acceptance over the years and lying in bed next to her thinking about the present and future alone, have I processed them enough not to let the emotions out, or am I just kidding myself? Will I be that stoic British guy who doesn't cry in the end? I guess I won't know until it happens.

Yesterday was another day of watching Janet with little energy and reading her face, which looked so uncomfortable and suffering. Am I the only one who sees it? She said her temples are feeling super sensitive, and I know she is blaming it on the cancer and wonders if the cancer has spread to her brain. Whatever it is, it seems to make her tired all the time. Plus, the itching continues, although the rash is gone. Lying in bed last night, she said that her liver hurts when she lies on her left side. All I can say is I'm sorry…. I know the decline is not going to be easy.

I try to write a poem:

> Seemingly out of nowhere, while I'm listening to music
> or walking in nature, scrolling fun videos of art, dance
> troupes, dogs, and laughing babies, it strikes like being
> hit in the face.
> With a splash of water out of the sink when doing the
> dishes, someone or something flips a switch.
> The unstoppable flow of emotion to the surface.
> It starts with a tear and then turns into sobs.
> Sometimes it lasts for 20 seconds and then it's gone,
> sometimes for five minutes.

It usually happens when I am alone, with no one to
comfort me, just me by myself. It starts as a feeling of joy
and quickly goes to sadness, then grief, then pain, and
then it's gone…momentary relief from the sadness of the
state of the planet.
Grief from the death and cancer, and pain from the
physical wear and tear of life.

Acceptance, compassion, love…. That is what it is like.

Day 13
Nov 24

I took a puff yesterday.... Why? I justified it by saying that I was feeling good and ok instead of wanting it to mask or hide my feelings.... You know, the denial thing.

Day 14
Nov 25

Last night, just as I was falling asleep, Janet finished reading, which is always half an hour after I fall asleep. She rolled over to spoon with me because that is the only way we can hold each other. Her hand landed on my penis, and she quickly pulled away and said, "I'm sorry." I said that it was ok, and she put it back. After a few minutes of very subtle movement on both our parts, it turned into the only way we can have anything that resembles making love at this point. This was a rare moment of sexual intimacy for us, and I welcomed it. I have accepted the lack of intimacy over the past years, resorting to masturbation for my sexual release. Most of the time, I am ok with that, but sometimes I end up feeling so lonely that I can barely handle it. Last night, as good as it felt to be touched by Janet, I felt so sad, guilty, and alone that I almost cried myself to sleep afterward. I don't think I can do that again. Janet is in too much discomfort and in a seemingly disconnected headspace all the time. I don't want to put her in a place of having to satisfy me sexually...or in any other way.

> *A Conversation about grief*
> *Can give you some temporary relief*
> *Domestication and programming lead to belief*
> *That life experience and trauma of pain*
> *Can bring us to a place of being insane*
> *When doing the same things and expecting different results*
> *Familiar triggers and similar insults*
> *Reinforced habits leading to pain*
> *Create problems and nothing to gain*

Chemical imbalance or environmental structure
Can send us down a determined juncture
Is it a choice or destiny for sure
When it feels like life is out of control
And the whole experience has taken its toll
"The winds will lift you up into the sky above
Where you'll be treated to memories you love"

Gratitude and appreciation of all the above, even the pain and struggle. Remember you can break the cycle of repeating and reinforced habits that take you down the rabbit hole.

Day 15
Nov 26

Pies, I love making pies! Particularly, apple pies with a puff pastry. Yesterday was a roller coaster. Feeling good, feeling bad, feeling good, feeling bad. The therapy session was good; it always goes by so quickly. Feeling bad about the reality of what was discussed, I tried to talk to Janet, which imploded quickly because she felt ganged up on when both Marlon and I asked her questions. Maybe instead of trying to talk to her, I will write the questions down, so I can have some clarity about her wishes for how to be taken care of as she declines. She doesn't want to talk or face the decline because the cancer is clearly killing her now. My pie crust came out perfect! Acceptance, compassion, and love, this is the practice and the challenge. Kaelan said that I was his rock. That was so kind of him to say so. It has been my life goal to live by the example of acceptance, compassion, and love. Maybe it will rub off on my kids. He is already such an amazing person.

Day 16
Nov 27

I've already done too much thinking this morning. My mind is racing about making pie and how run-down Janet is. We were really concerned about her driving to her mom's house by herself yesterday for Thanksgiving. She made it all right. She is winded all the time now, and the "chemo brain" has become a real mind fog. She hasn't opened her mail in a very long time and forgets things a lot more now. Is this the real decline? Or a temporary setback? The proton radiation sounds so promising and can't come soon enough. I am afraid Janet isn't going to make it to her 60th birthday in March or Tim's wedding in June. There is a fine line between not only discussing what is coming but also preparing for it psychologically and physically. This sucks, I don't like it at all! It's all-consuming and difficult not to think about all the time…. I guess I'll make the pie now.

Day 17
Nov 28

I took a walk when I got to Janet's mom's home in Essex.
By myself. I feel like I need to tell Karen, Lena, and Dana
my opinion and concern about where Janet is right now. It's
kind of a fine line. She isn't sick from the flu, or Covid, or a
bad cold. You can see that her energy is depleted. She is out
of breath and says her abdomen hurts when she walks up the
stairs, one step at a time. Definitely not able to go for the
walks around the neighborhood here in Essex like we used to.
The color of her skin is more olive than usual, and her face is
more puffy. It seems like it's getting harder for her to pull her
thoughts together when she is talking. I am becoming more
seriously concerned that this is the beginning of the cancer
decline and that maybe I should be sharing my concerns with
select people. It might piss her off.

She said a couple of things recently when I brought up some of
my concerns: "I don't trust anyone," and "I feel like I am being
ganged up on." I don't know why she feels like she doesn't trust
anyone. I'm sure the ganged-up feeling came from when Marlon
and I shared with her our concerns about her tiredness and overall
demeanor.

Other thoughts while I was walking the neighborhood: How
to pay for things at the end? Hospice, cremation, the memorial
service. I really need to be clear about Janet's wishes, but she
shuts down quickly when I bring up any of these things.
Understandably, she doesn't want to face these thoughts and
decisions. Over the past five years of holidays and special events,

I/we always felt that it could be the last holiday together, but this time I feel that this probably will be the last holiday together. I don't know if Janet is going to make it to the New Year's, her birthday, Tim's wedding… for real. All very serious stuff on my mind most of the time. I guess that's the way it is when you are going through it with a loved one. How weird will it be when she is gone? her mom is still playing tennis at 84, and Janet is so sick with cancer at 59! It's hard to make any sense out of it.

Last spring, after her near-death experience due to the cupping, she recovered and got better and stronger as time passed. It was slow going, but there was improvement from day to day, in her will, her ability to eat, walk, work, talk, and go places. Now it's the reverse. Instead of the "rebound," it's the "decline." It's really hard to watch and be positive. Acceptance, compassion, and love more than ever before. It's a matter of making the right decisions at the right time. But will I be able to do that?

Janet is starting to wake up. Lois is pulling out the plates and starting to prep for the day. I hear talking in the other room, my phone starts to buzz, so here we go…Thanksgiving Day 2024.

Day 18
Nov 29

I forgot to take my pee meds yesterday, so it was harder to feel my pee this morning. Now that makes me feel old!

It was great to see and be with Dagan on Thanksgiving. He is doing well, and I am truly happy for him. Janet and Marlon cooked most of the meal. She pushed through her tiredness, although I could see her slumping and holding herself up all day. I cooked the turkey down the road, so I was able to speak with Karen on the phone and update her on my opinion about Janet's apparent decline. I am beginning to hate that word, decline, and what it represents in my life. The itching has gotten really bad, all over her body. last night, it drove Janet to tears. Christmas is the next milestone to get to, then her 60th birthday at the end of March, Tim's wedding in June, and Aja's wedding in August. Come on, proton radiation therapy, you can't come soon enough!

Matthew, open your mail!!!

Day 19
Nov 30

Natasha, Remony, and Phyllida came for visits with Janet today. I am so happy they did because Janet was really struggling earlier in the day. I have been feeling that it is really important for her that people visit because if the decline happens fast, these will be "last visits." That is what the "Janet World Tour" was all about two years ago: visiting old friends for what might be the very last time. What a good and easy trip that was. I will always remember it as such. The Viking cruise trip this past October was also good, but it was hard work for all of us.
I raised some red flags to Remony and Phyllida, and they made the trip happen even though they were busy taking care of their dad. I am grateful to Natasha, who came and took Janet out to lunch. I also have talked to Kenny because I know Janet loves him a lot and would appreciate a visit with him as well. I will also reach out to Suzy and Dana.

Day 20
Dec 2

My "normal" and "routine" have changed. Janet is now ill all
the time and reacts with greater intensity when I ask her basic
questions like: Are you hungry? Or: Can I make you dinner?
Or: How are you feeling? Or, or, or… I need to take my own
advice and not take it personally, but it's very hard for this to be
the new normal. I would rather not ask her anything than have
her respond so aggressively. Who knows how I would react if I
were feeling what she is feeling all the time now? Itchy all over,
upset stomach, run down, tired, overwhelmed with thinking or
answering questions…and scared of dying. Maybe not scared of
dying, but not knowing how the cancer is progressing and how
much time she has left in this world. It's difficult to think about
it when your body is "normal" and feeling ok, but to add the
physical and psychological struggle with cancer ailments really
fucking sucks! I am feeling numb, so to speak, when it comes
to thinking about being able to do anything for her. I definitely
can't ease the discomfort or struggle.

I think of the short story I wrote, "She Plays the Game," when
Janet was dealing with her nerve sheath tumor seven years ago,
and spent all her time addicted to the phone to distract herself
from the constant pain. All I can do is "carry on." Wait… for
what? For her to die?

The insurance company has refused to pay for the proton radiation therapy, and I am hoping the doctors can rally for its ap-
proval so they can try one last thing to save Janet's life. If
and when they start the treatment, will she have the strength

to endure how her body reacts to the therapy? When will the time come when she accepts that this is the real beginning of the end? It's hard to write about my daily stuff when Janet is experiencing such suffering.

Day 21
Dec 3

Today would've been Andrew's birthday. I spoke about him and my last experience with him to my therapist yesterday. Of all the end-of-life experiences, this one presses my emotional buttons the most as I recalled Lena and me visiting him in the hospital and seeing how his body had deteriorated. I couldn't help but cry talking about it. And then I wept after speaking with Dana on the phone about Janet. This is hard going through what feels like the end of life of my beloved. There are fine lines between honoring her and giving her the space to be and feel without imposing my wants: for her to feel better, to be "normal," to eat properly, to rest, to share her thoughts and feelings, and to talk to me. Acceptance, compassion, and love without trying to impose my will. It is only with love and compassion that I have such deep concern for her well-being, and that she is struggling so much that I would say anything at all. Small shifts in her reactions and what looks like her acceptance. It's all encompassing with my thoughts and hard to shake.

Marlon is doing the grocery shopping. TLC meeting tomorrow morning for my art to be displayed at the restaurant. Rick the plumber is coming to snake out the big house kitchen sink. I am going to Phish with Dagan at the end of the month. It's hard to go on with "life as normal" when she is so sick.

Day 22
Dec 4

Proctalgia Fugax! Butt ache is no fun!!!

What do I have to write about today? Janet, cancer, the all-encompassing thoughts, and all the seriousness of how it is going to play out? It's very hard not to project into the future. Just being present here now is virtually impossible because of always being on guard for the emergency of rapid decline, to be ready to make the necessary decisions. I pushed myself to sleep in until 7:30 this morning just to feel the warmth of her feet and to hear her breathing.

Day 23
Dec 5

I have my annual physical today. It snowed.

Janet rested all day and slept a lot. Her body itching is really driving her mad. She is now making these small noises. I'm not sure if she knows or cares that she is making them, and I can't really describe them… maybe grunts or groans? I feel terrible for her. It's so hard to watch her go through this. She meets with the MSK dermatologist today in the city, a solo trip, which I know is going to be exhausting for her big time.

I just peed and had kidney pain on my left side. That's three times in the last 10 days or so. Kidney pain sucks! But watching what Janet has and continues to go through, I make sure I don't complain about any of my physical ailments: my joint and bone aches, my difficulty breathing and coughing, and the dry skin on my face.

Day 24
Dec 6

Kaelan just left. He spent the night here after coming to the
Mandala art opening I had last night. What a surprise! I didn't
expect to see him. The opening was fun. Marlon, Kaelan, Beth,
and nine others made it out. I shared some stories and laughs;
it was good. Janet was too tired to make it after her trip to NYC
and was asleep by the time we got home at 8:15. I stopped her
from scratching her skin off at 5 a.m. What an awful sound.
She is supposed to work this morning. I have a feeling this
weekend will be her last days on the job.

She never did take that trip she always wanted to with just her
and Marlon to the west coast. How can Ken and Lois help?
The question and the answer hover over me every day. Fourteen
days 'til Karen and Karl show up. Kaelan and Manda will come
to Essex for Christmas Day dinner, which will be good. Nineteen
days away. I am worried that Janet will be too run-down and
exhausted by then. What a weird thing to think about…the
normalcy of Christmas, Phish concerts, winter, and spring not
being normal because of cancer and or death. FUCK!!!

Day 25
Dec 7

Last night I had moments of internal struggle thinking that I cannot handle witnessing Janet suffering with this itchy body anymore. I can't imagine myself going through what she is going through. I wouldn't want to live anymore. Sometimes I see it on her face; it's terrible. The dermatologist says she has "Red itchy spot disease." OBVIOUSLY!!!! There is no relief from the incessant itching. I held onto her hands for a few minutes. She said the sensation of intense itch jumped around her body—leg, chest, head, forearm, shoulder, face—until she pulled her hands away and couldn't resist any more. It's constant. From my perspective, just try to distract the mind, watch TV, or try to super meditate and focus your attention on the breath or something else, not the body. Again, there is nothing I can do to give her any sense of relief, so I must accept and love her with compassion…or remove myself and take a break with a walk; otherwise, I will go crazy watching her itch her skin off. The THC gummies seem to help when she goes to bed. Sleep is the only relief she gets. She even scratched me in the middle of the night. It freaked me out.

Suzy and Nancy are both coming to spend a little time with Janet at different times today.

Day 26
Dec 10

Everyone I tell about what we're going through says, "It's a lot." Apparently, for someone else…it is a lot! To me, it just is. It's who and what I am at the moment. Doing, moving, making, not much "downtime." I don't even know what downtime is. Sitting? Reading? Watching TV? Scrolling?

Keep writing. This is the hard practice for me, writing, probably because there is so much thinking involved. It doesn't take much thinking to walk. Yes, there is some while I walk, but thinking about what I am going to put on the page is different. Writing with intention. "I'll write this sentence next. I'll write this sentence next. I'll write this sentence next. I'll write this sentence next. I'll write this sentence next. I'll write this sentence next. I'll write this sentence next. I'll write this sentence next. I'll write this sentence next. I'll write this sentence next. I'll write this sentence next. I'll write this sentence next. I'll write this sentence next. I'll write this sentence next. I'll write this sentence next. I'll write this sentence next. I'll write this sentence next. I'll write this sentence next. I'll write this sentence next. I'll write this sentence next." Sip of coffee… I'll write this sentence next. I'll write this sentence next. I'll write this sentence next. I'll write this sentence next. I'll write this sentence next. I'll write this sentence next. I'll write this sentence next. I'll write this sentence next. I'll write this sentence next. I'll write this sentence next. I'll write this sentence next. I'll write this sentence next. I'll write this sentence next. I'll write this sentence next. I'll write this sentence next.

Day 27
Dec 12

Janet is getting sicker and weaker by the day. I drove her to her meeting with Dana yesterday. Dana now realizes how far along Janet is with the cancer because she was so out of breath just from walking up the stairs at the studio. Janet really wants to keep working because she doesn't like being sick at home on the couch, but she is so exhausted all the time. And what an awful thing with her full body itching! It's enough to drive anyone completely insane, and it's really hard to witness. The human body experience really sucks sometimes, and now I think maybe all the time for Janet. Where is the joy? Where is the relief? Where is the peace? Definitely not here on Earth. I'm not sure what else to say....

Day 28
Dec 13

So much sleep. Janet woke up at noon to go to Mount Kisco with me. It took her two hours to get ready. A shower and a full body rubdown by Marlon, and I to try to help with the itching. Janet slept in the car, then she slept some more before dinner. She stayed awake for a movie and then fell asleep for the night. We did talk a little about where to have a memorial service for her. At first, she thought at the Clark Funeral Home in Katonah because it's close to the train station and convenient for people. But she really wants it to be at the Yoga Loft at the Bedford Post. We also talked about friends visiting, but she was reluctant to make any concrete plans because she feels like she wouldn't be able to talk much. Then she asked Marlon what dates they plan to be in Lisbon and said, "Maybe I'll meet you there." Marlon's response was, "That would be great." We know by now there is no way Janet could make such a trip.

I am driving her to work again this morning. It's really fucking cold out. In my mind, I've been preparing for, as Janet would say, "waiting for the shoe to drop," with thoughts of a memorial service and what I would say, and how I would post about her death on Facebook. How we would deal with her body and cremation, and how to pay for it all? Do I start making arrangements now? What about hospice? And who does the "declaration of death"? What happens next? What will I do? What will Marlon do? Things are not so simple leading up to the death of your beloved. Picking the right time to speak of these things while Janet is still able. Maybe I should have another conversation with Karen, who has her "power of attorney."

Day 29
Dec 15

Another roller-coaster ride! Janet was thoroughly drained and slept on and off on the couch all day and couldn't muster the strength to go see *Shakey Graves* with Marlon at the Capital Theater. So I went instead. The day before, Janet was able to go to work from 9 to 3 and then go with me to the art supply store in Norwalk. It was good because there was almost a sense of normalcy. Today I hope she just wakes up; she is supposed to work all day today.

The good news is that the insurance company finally approved the proton radiation therapy! This Friday, I will take her to the center in Harlem, where they will do an MRI and make a body cast; it's a full-day event. Then the treatment will start in January. I really hope Janet makes it 'til then, even though we don't know how her body will react or what the side effects will be.

Shakey Graves was fun for Marlon. Unfortunately, Janet's looming death changes everything for me. To know that at any minute or any day could be the end, and how life will change so much for me and Marlon. Yet, we still make plans to have some sense of normalcy: Christmas, the Phish concert, Marlon's Europe trip—all still to come—as well as the new treatment. I am feeling old.... And tired.

Day 30
Dec 16

I am so grateful for all four of my kids. I feel close to them all; we respect each other and have relationships built on trust. How lucky am I? Today: therapy at 11, walk, read, put out the garbage, make beef stew....

Day 31
Dec 17

I took Janet to get her pump flushed at 4 p.m. I had to wake her up and help her get ready at 3… so much sleeping! As we got in the car, she looked at me with the saddest face and asked me, "When can I stop doing this?" Meaning, when can I stop living? I said, "When you are ready to." Then, while we were in the waiting room at MSK, she asked, "How can anyone go on like this?" Questioning how she can possibly go on feeling the way she does—this is no way to live…. I feel so terrible for her, seeing her body strength diminish and her mental strength deteriorate. I can see how hard it is for her to think about the answers to basic questions and to formulate her thoughts. This really sucks. Covid test today so she can get ready for the proton radiation prep on Friday. Meets with her oncologist on Thursday at 3, and Chris at 11. All things that will be difficult to get her to.

There is a familiar sense of numbness around all this experience. I guess it is a similar feeling to when Mom and Dad were in transition, leading up to their deaths. Just trying to handle each thing or issue as they come, the best way possible, without too much emotional release. Although the emotional release comes at the oddest times. Writing helps, taking walks definitely helps, therapy helps, staying busy always helps, talking it out helps. Sometimes when I am busy with other things, I think to myself, "What am I doing not focusing 100% on Janet and what is to come with logistical details? Is that guilt? Or is it just coping with the situation? Ok, she's awake.

Day 32
Dec 18

I just re-read the Thanksgiving Day entry, and things are still declining…. Yesterday I spoke with Lena, Karen, Dana, and texted with Chris about my concerns and my opinion. Memorial service, cremation, hospice, all things I want to be prepared for, especially the hospice care. I have emailed the social worker at MSK for advice and found out that there is a Vitas in Fairfield County, the same hospice organization that helped with Mom and Dad in Florida. The ball is rolling now. When will the time be right to speak with Janet? She spoke with the proton radiation people yesterday about the procedure prep on Friday and what to expect, as well as a social worker who gave her the option of staying in the city during the 15 days of treatment. The catch is that the treatment is on 126th Street in Harlem, and the place to stay is near Penn Station in mid-town. To get from point A to point B even today would be really hard for her, so I am not sure if that will work. I just want to get through today, tomorrow, Friday, and this weekend. Christmas is a week away. I really want people to visit her. Dana, Suzy, Taylor, Nancy, Kenny, Karen, Karl, maybe Gretchen.

Day 33
Dec 19

We broke down together when we went to bed last night. Janet is too sick to carry on! Suffering so much. The itching and throwing up last night were so terrible. I really hope she decides not to go through with the proton radiation and let these end days unfold as they will. The insurance weighs so heavily on her, concerned that her work doesn't want to pay the $800/month anymore. She got that email just before she went to bed.

The oncologist meeting yesterday was the reality check that I needed. There are no more treatments that can be done. The response after asking the doctor if she thought the proton radiation would do any good was that she felt it would help to relieve the symptoms that Janet is experiencing due to the cancer tumor having grown. I say BULLSHIT! She doesn't know the extent of Janet's exhaustion and itching. And how hard it will be to get to and from treatment each day. "There is nothing else to be done!" So the doctor is going to send some links for the MSK palliative care. Those words are just as hard to hear as the word hospice. Basically, medication to relieve pain, going into and through hospice. Friday: proton radiation prep, MRI, CT scan. Then decide to do it or not?

Last night, Janet was done and didn't want to wake up today. She doesn't want to go to her mom's for Christmas. She just wants to go to sleep with me and Marlon and not wake up. I couldn't keep it together…. It all broke me! THIS SUCKS!!!!

Day 34
Dec 21

I'm at Sticks and Stones retreat center—Beth leading a meditation and me leading a drum circle to honor the Winter Solstice. Release of the fear. What fear…? Letting go. "What are the thresholds of today and what is possible now?" Always a life-and-death threshold being a caregiver for Janet, and the balance of living each day and planning some enjoyment tomorrow. Is it a balance or is it what is, just what is? Will life ever not be "a lot," as everyone keeps saying about my experience? Do I like it being "a lot"? Am I addicted to it? The threshold? Past the threshold, there is letting go and peace. Support and love. People to lean on. Organizations to tap into to make it all a bit easier…. LET'S DRUM!

Day 35
Dec 23

Too cold for humans outside today! Janet's body itching was too much even for me last night. I am amazed she hasn't gone crazy because of it. I have had conversations with two other people who were caregivers for their partners with liver failure, who had passed away, and both said that their bodies itched all the way to the end as well. It's been a bad month… unbearable for Janet, almost unbearable for me to witness.

We finished watching all the extended versions of Lord of the Rings over a week. What an incredible creation of fantasy. I could watch it over and over. Drumming was good on Saturday with Beth. I made myself vulnerable with what I said about Janet's acceptance, compassion, as well as the usual healing vibrations of the community drumming. I often think of all the people going through or have gone through what I am going through, and do find some comfort in it. It was great to see Karen, Karl, and Tim yesterday and to have them witness a little of what Janet is going through, and for me to see them and Janet reacting to each other.

Day 36
Dec 24

This has turned into a journal more than just the "morning pages" of mumbo jumbo, which was the original intention when I began to write every day.

Today, I make chicken soup in the hope that Janet will eat it. I feel it is my job to make sure she has food available to eat. Yesterday, she wanted to go to the dispensary in White Plains to get a particular brand of gummies for gifts. And then to Target to look for specific gifts for her mom and Marlon. Mostly to get out of the house and off the couch. Going to the dispensary wasn't so bad; she stayed in the car. But the drive to Target was crazy because of how many people were trying to get to the store. Janet was feeling terrible, but was determined to do this. As we walked inside, the lines to check out were all the way to the far end of the store; there was no way we were going to wait. So, we walked to where Janet thought the items were. We walked very slowly as I held her arm; she looked so weak and sick. All of a sudden, she realized that it had been a very long time since she was in Target, and I think that really bummed her out. We got back in the car to go to the grocery store, and she threw up the entire way there. Still determined to go in, maybe one last time, who knows? She threw up the entire way home, too. Good thing I had some MSK barf bags in the glove box. To me, the pre-barf cough sounds like it's coming from her lungs and getting worse.

When we got home, she immediately fell into a deep sleep on the couch. At least she isn't itching her skin off when she is asleep.

Before we went out, she let me put the Sarna anti-itch cream all over her body, which I believe is helpful. Hopefully, just having my loving hands on her body gives her a small sense of relief. I know it feels good for me to connect with her in that way.

Day 37
Dec 28

This is really hard! It's hard to take care of myself, but it's really fucking hard to take care of someone else, even if it is your partner. I always think I am doing the right thing for Janet, and all of a sudden, she gets upset with me and says, "Do you ever take my wishes into consideration?" I drove her to the yoga studio yesterday from 8 to 12 after two days in Essex, visiting with family. She decided at the last minute, at 2 in the afternoon on Christmas Day, that she wanted to be there. After work, she came home and slept on the couch. I managed to get some soup in her... but she coughed and threw up a lot before bed—along with moaning and groaning all night long. Before going to sleep, she springs on me that she wants to go to work again on Saturday and Sunday.... Whaaat? I have secretly arranged for the "core four" high school friends to come here at noon today for maybe a "final visit."

Telemedicine Zoom meeting with the oncologist's assistant on Thursday, which was helpful for me to understand her coughing and hacking. The tumor putting pressure on the bile duct doesn't allow the bile to move, which needs to come up instead of down. They might have to put in a stent to help with that, but it means another surgery, which would put off the proton radiation even further. Janet's bilirubin numbers are so high that we have to keep an eye on the yellowing of the whites of her eyes and maybe bring her to the MSK emergency room, especially if she gets a fever, all of which would postpone the proton therapy. She wants to go to work because she feels like she is withering away...dying in this house....

Phish TONIGHT!!!

Day 38
Dec 29

I made it to *Phish* at Madison Square Garden…. Amazing! It was hard not to think about what Janet is going through as I looked around the crowd, knowing that Janet wasn't ever going to experience live music again. A mother/daughter team sat behind us. I appreciate that Dagan and I have our bond of love for music, especially *Phish* shows. We are so lucky to have the music we love, that the band we love is still playing after 40 years, and that we have the ability to do that together. Very special and cherished by both of us.

Gretchen, Allison, Margaret, and Nancy came to visit Janet for three and a half hours yesterday. I was a bit nervous because I didn't ask or tell her that they were coming. She was still in bed at noon when they arrived, and they surrounded her with love. I could tell Janet was sad after they left, with the realization that it wasn't going to get any better and that she wanted to spend more time with them. She really enjoyed the stories and memories they all shared and looking at pictures together. She was blown away that Gretchen came from Maine and Allison flew in from Indianapolis just to visit her. How important it was to have them here when Janet is still coherent and able to have conversations and hug them. It was good for all of them and meant the world to Janet and me that they came…when they came.

Day 39
Jan 2, 2025

Yesterday was very hard. All sorts of signs that the end is getting closer for Janet. She didn't know what date it was. She was in bed til 4 p.m. She was hacking a lot. She said a few things like, "Why am I enduring this?" and "I am 100% depleted of energy." Which is why she is moaning and groaning and making little whimpering sounds. At one point, she barely had the energy to roll over in bed when Marlon and I were gently brushing her skin. We finally had her get up to take a shower, checking on her every couple of minutes, and when she turned off the water, I went in to help her. She was in the tub on her hands and knees because it took too much energy and was hard for her to stand. I helped her out, and we put anti-itch lotion on her. I helped dress her so she could be on the couch when her friend Kenny came to visit. They visited for an hour and a half, which was good for everyone. Marlon finally convinced her to eat some oatmeal with apple, but only because I was "pestering" her for not taking her meds—if she doesn't eat, she won't make it to the proton therapy date on the 9th. Then she said to us that there will come a time when she will ask us not to take care of her any-more, meaning not to feed her or make sure she is taking meds.... Making her comfortable and loving her up will happen all the way to the end.

I am worried about her over the next week. I think she is going to be too sick for treatment. She still wants us to take her to the studio on Friday and Sunday! I don't think Marlon should go on their trip to Europe. This is all so fuckin hard!!! On a positive note, I ended up going to see *Phish* all 4 nights with Dagan. It was great! Definitely my church. I have so much gratitude for so many reasons: that Marlon and Janet pushed me to go, that I can see the spontaneous improv music I love so much being played by a band that is healthy and happy and going strong after 40 years. Grateful for the massive communal experience of 20,000 people dancing and singing together, who all love the experience like I do. Super high energy at various points and amazing, loving, philosophical lyrics that have personal meaning to each and every one of us in the audience.

On the night of the 30th, I experienced a connection to the divine source of love that brought me to tears of joy. A lot of tears, many times. At one point, I turned away from the band to see the crowd with lights on all of us during a high-energy point—beautiful colors of the people, and the space around us filled with bubbles.... I felt so good, and it was so beautiful, I imagined and felt that I was at the gates of heaven. That is what I will experience just before I pass to the next realm. At that moment, something told me that everything is going to be ok, even when we die.

And then on the 31st, during the song "Stash," I experienced an outburst of extreme grief and sadness while I was dancing, and I broke down into uncontrollable sobs. I allowed them to come and was aware of what it must've looked like to the people around me, and I still allowed it to happen. And then I felt Dagan's hand on my back, knowing and comforting me all the while the band played, the people danced...the grief exploded... THANK YOU!!!!

Day 40
Jan 3

Kaelan came for a visit yesterday. He seriously offered that I live with him and Manda if my property managing gig falls through. That wasn't expected at all. If that happened, it would be temporary, and there are so many other things to consider, but what an amazing thing for a child to offer his father! I feel blessed to have such incredible support from my children.

Janet was forced to get up yesterday at noon because Dana came over to visit and talk about work. I think it was good for Dana to see Janet in person and be able to gauge how sick she really is. I bought a shower chair and a wheelchair for Janet. She wasn't happy about that. She was awake for the rest of the day because Kaelan was setting up a new TV sound system. Awesome!! After he left, Janet and I sat on the couch holding each other.

Better night's sleep last night. Six days till treatment. Janet is going to go to the studio two more times, today and Sunday, with Marlon's help; and then going on "leave" till the end of February.

Day 41
Jan 4

I slept on the couch in the hope that Janet could get a better
night's sleep without me tossing and turning and keeping her
awake. It was a rough night for me. Janet did a lot yesterday.
She went to the studio with Marlon and then to Westport;
dealt with health insurance, MSK portal, radiation portal,
answering questions; ate fried chicken; and watched TV.
I scratched her down a couple of times, which felt good for
both of us. I spoke with Grace Cottage Hospital in Vermont
about the MAID process and spoke with Karen for a while.
I also spoke with Chrisy from the radiation center about the
Hope Lodge. It felt like a productive day.

Five days til radiation. I think Janet is actually going to make it.
She has a PET scan on Monday and a Telemed with dermatology.
I can't believe how much snot is coming out of my nose.

Day 42
Jan 7

At MSK right now for Janet's PET scan. I have accepted that I will be sleeping on the couch from now on. Admittedly, I think we are both getting better sleep. I am looking around at all the people who are here by themselves. Janet is lucky to have me with her all the time for the past five-and-a-half years. It would be dreadful to have to go through all this by yourself, for sure. We are both psychologically preparing for the treatment in the city, going to Hope Lodge tomorrow night, and the logistics of being in and out and up and down Manhattan. Karen is coming on Sunday. Wouldn't it be something if the treatments work and Janet gets better! I was thinking about how my life has been put on "hold" this past year since last year's near-death experience. It's very hard to think about the future.

Listening to a short podcast called "Remember The Soul," a documentary series by Joe Plante.

> *What is this teaching me and you*
> *Make sense out of suffering*
> *Of the seemingly terminal illness*
> *Of Janet and the entire planet*
> *The soul lessons and the understanding*
> *Of the suffering and pain*
> *The struggle to stay alive in these bodies*
> *Knowing that peace and love*
> *Is there in the end.*

Look at all the people wanting to stay in their bodies, not only here but all over the planet.

Day 43
Jan 8

I thought last night was it. I sat with Janet on the bed for a while after she wretched for an hour and was almost too exhausted to get up from the bathroom floor. I watched…I listened and held her as her breath slowed to almost not…like the last day of Mom and Dad. Her body is shutting down. I can see it and feel it.

The proton radiation doctor called, saying that the cancer has spread to the left side of the liver and that the bile duct obstruction was a problem. He gave me mixed messages. He wanted to delay the treatment to Jan 13 and lower the dose because the cancer tumor is so close to the skin now, and he was afraid the radiation would really change her skin. He said he couldn't talk because he was supposed to be in a clinic, and he needed to confer with the oncologist about how to proceed. The process and the lack of attention and communication have been so bad that it has literally cost Janet's life. I feel that the oncologist's team gave up on her after the last chemo treatment on Sept 30 and the last scan on October 20. More than three months of nothing but cancer spreading and lack of attention from the "team."

I wish Janet would let go of her body now. She has suffered so much these past couple of months with the itching, the retching, the exhaustion, and the nausea, along with the internal discomfort. I see it in her eyes, the same way I saw it in Elisa's eyes before she passed. Janet hasn't eaten in a couple of days. Yesterday, she didn't take her meds at all. The moaning and groaning in the middle of the night was almost too much for me to bear.

Day 44
Jan 15

It's been hard for me to bring myself to write this past week. Logistics have been hard for me. The last day I wrote, I broke down emotionally and didn't think I could carry on with all of this. I called Lena and Michael in the morning, and they arrived in New Canaan in the evening. Karen changed her plans and arrived the next morning to help with treatments, to stay at Hope Lodge with Janet, and to help with logistics.

After the first two treatments, Janet came home to rest for the weekend. We all had our hands on her over the weekend, rubbing her feet, scratching the never-ending itches, and holding her hand. Sunday, Ken and Lois visited for most of the day, which was good. I spent time with Ken away from the house so that Lois, Karen, and Marlon could spend time with Janet. I think that Lois finally got it that Janet is going to die soon. When she left, she gave me a long hug, and I could sense her crying some.

Dana came over with Babka that her son Nate made and held Janet's hand for half an hour. Then Marlon, Karen, Janet, and I crafted a post for Facebook explaining what was happening with Janet and a link to a donation page. Wow, the response has been amazing. Sixty people have donated to make the fund more than 18 thousand dollars! Along with prayers and love. So at the moment, I feel very supported by friends and family. Ken and Lois brought us cash for basic expenses as well. Karen is with Janet in the city at Hope Lodge and treatments, while Marlon and I recuperate for the final hurrah. This week has been unbelievable.

Day 45
Jan 17

Trying to write before going to bed. Today was hard…feeling like this past week was a trial run for being here in the house without Janet. Karen is still in the city with her at Hope Lodge. I feel like things are slowing down here. It's 8 p.m. and I'm already in bed. Today I walked in the rain. Painted some rocks. Watched some TV, ate, cleaned dishes, and drank a lot of coffee. Trying to allow the feelings to come and go. We FaceTimed with Janet and Karen, and it reminded me how sick she is. I really miss the healthy Janet a lot! Feeling her in bed next to me and hearing her breathe…I am already lonely. Am I/we ready for the final leg of this journey? Can you ever be ready? It's supposed to snow tomorrow…. Oh well.

Day 46
Jan 23

Fuckin cold out! I brought Janet and Marlon home from Hope Lodge last night. Her last treatment was on the 21st, and she is not looking so good. When Kaelan and I visited her there on the 19th, she looked like she wasn't in as much discomfort from the week before, but she isn't looking good now. They said she will be super tired from the radiation for a while. The roller coaster ride continues. Not a very good quality of life…maybe that will change. It seems like a waiting game now.

Day 47
Jan 24

I slept better last night on the couch. Janet and I had some beautiful moments yesterday. Just sitting, holding each other, talking, and falling asleep together. She was verbalizing who I should fall in love with after she is gone. And when she went to bed, I put lotion on her entire body, warmed up her side of the bed, and knelt to hold her and say, "I love you." She said, "It'll be over soon, and that's ok." It's an odd feeling and sensation to see her bones in her arms and shoulders so pronounced now.

It's interesting to see what she craves to eat at night. Last night it was grilled cheese on rye bread with a pickle and tomato. I drove to Danbury to get her the special Sonic ice she discovered while in the city to have with her Mexican Coke. She loves the ice with her chocolate Ensure protein drink…. And Coke! No one would have ever seen that coming from Janet. She is very weak in her legs, and her muscle mass has noticeably diminished. She tried stretching a little before she went to bed and was moaning because it was so hard for her. She wants to go somewhere warm in February, so we are tossing around a basic plan to go to Florida…? That would be something.

Day 48
Jan 25

Janet looked so sad when she went to bed last night. A deep sadness that I have not seen on her face before. I helped her into bed, undressed her, and put her pajamas on her. Putting cream on her dry skin and noticing the thinness of her arms and bones, as well as her weakness due to the lack of muscle. I can see that she doesn't want the help, but I sense that when she looks in the mirror, she sees the end of life coming, and it makes her so sad... deeply sad. I make sure she hears me say, "I love you and take me with you into your dreams." I kiss her gently on her bony cheek and forehead. When will she let go fully?

Lois will come to visit today and tomorrow. Karen and Karl are on their way to Seattle to prepare for Tim's wedding. Marlon is walking the dogs and staying close. Janet talks of wanting to go somewhere warm. Southern California is on fire, and it's snowing in Atlanta and northern Florida. I am not sure if it's the right time to take her somewhere now. I honestly don't know if she would make it.... I am waiting.

Day 49
Jan 27

Waking up with a headache is no fun. I am tired of sleeping on the couch. I do love tucking Janet into bed at night. I warm up her side of the bed while she is brushing her teeth. I put cream on her belly and back, and we talk gently. I put my face against her cheek, kiss her forehead, and say, "Take me with you into your dreams." Same routine every night. Making sure she has taken her Gas-X and Mucinex and has plenty of water and tissues on both sides of the bed. "Good night, Janet. I love you so much."

Ken and Lois visited both Saturday and Sunday. Janet says that it's a lot but also wants the conversational interaction. I made room in our small house by going to the movies while they were here...saw The Brutalist. It was pretty good, but it was no Dune. Kimberly came to visit and to be the notary for some of Janet's paperwork. Ken came and went. Lois and Marlon went for walks, all trying to be respectful of Janet's need for rest.

Day 50
Jan 28

I slept for 10 hours, and heard Janet cough at around 3 a.m.

Yesterday felt like an upswing for her. She was awake most of
the day, spoke with the doctor to discuss the bile duct stent
scheduled for tomorrow, if it happens. We still have not heard
from the radiation doctor or the oncologist! Suzy came for a visit,
which was great as usual. I started a new art piece—first time
in months. I'll call it "Bathroom floor," because that's what it
reminds me of when I look at it. I reserved tattoo time on
March 1 for Aja and Kaelan's birthday. Wow, time is a weird
thing. A month ago, I thought Janet was going to die soon, and
here we still are, and planning to go to another surgery.
Maybe she will make it to 60 after all.

Day 51
Jan 30

Time for another video diary. Janet is down to 103 pounds now.
Her bones are very noticeable. She was 117 pounds when she went
for the proton radiation treatment on the 9th. I've noticed that
she is stuttering a bit, and it's sometimes hard for her to form her
sentences. Natalie came to massage her feet again yesterday.
Ken and Lois will come again today, and Natasha will come on
Sunday. This process is hard. I visited with Leslie and Greg
yesterday and explained what Janet is going through and how it
all feels very "practical" right now. The ups and downs happen,
and the downs can definitely feel overwhelming, but the way I was
talking about it feels "practical." The death with dignity or MAID,
and the process in Vermont—it amazes me how many people
don't know about it. I am excited about Aja and Kaelan's birthday
weekend at the end of February. I wonder if Janet will still be alive
then? When I tucked her in last night, she said, "I don't think I am
going to die tonight, so I'll see you in the morning."

9:30 p.m.: Janet said I am making her feel uncomfortable in
this house! Because I reacted to her tone of voice when she said
she didn't have enough money to have Natalie come and massage
her feet every week. I am really fuckin tired of this shit! I had a
couple of "reactive" stress moments today. One was about not
having enough chocolate chips to make cookies, and the other
was general frustration around the mess in the kitchen.
YES, I WANT TO RUN AWAY!!! She can go back to being
really sick again and probably will…. I am doing my best.

Day 52
Jan 31

Be careful what you say, Matthew. The better Janet feels, the less control she has over the tone of her voice and the aggressiveness of what she is saying. It's really hard not to react in a negative way. My saying, "You don't have to be upset with me," then gets interpreted as me taking it personally, and that makes her feel bad. She seems annoyed with me for taking care of her the way I do. Maybe I DO need to remove myself from the picture? Am I being selfish when I say I feel like I want to run away from this situation?

There is no "getting better." There is only enduring till the end. How am I going to go on without feeling and showing my resentment and my grumpiness? Janet painted such a rosy picture of herself yesterday in front of the doctor. Meanwhile, she looked like she was on death's door a couple of hours earlier, while she was sitting in her chair. I guess this is the type of roller coaster hell for me too. Sorry, I can't be positive and happy all the time...FUCK!!!

Day 53
Feb 2

Instead of Janet and Marlon just explaining the details that
I have "forgotten" or didn't know, they get upset with me for
not remembering. Which definitely makes me feel like shit, not
only for not remembering but because of their tone of voice....
I guess it's just another example of me taking what they say
personally. The last time, I recognized how I was feeling but only
reacted with "ok" and didn't say how much it bothered me.
Yet another example of me not wanting to be here, because I seem
to be upsetting Janet for not remembering.

It's so cold outside. Nancy came to visit today. Apparently, Janet
says she worries more about me than Marlon after she is gone....
Why? It's really hard for me to be in this house right now, and it's
really hard being away from this house right now....

Day 54
Feb 5

I took Janet to MSK Harrison last night to have her pump flushed. We were there for two-and-a-half hours for a 15-minute procedure. Janet was able to walk in and out on her own accord, and she was very engaging with the floor nurses. As she gave the attending nurse a big and long hug when she was done, I thought to myself, "I wonder if this is the last time they will see each other?" Today I am going to make gluten-free chocolate chip cookies

.

Day 55
Feb 6

FUCK THIS!!!!!

Day 56
Feb 7

It's very hard for me not to take some of the shit Janet says personally. Yesterday was rough. I am really doing the best I can here. The thing that hurt the most is that she said I haven't asked or don't ask her how she is doing! She says her friends have—how she is deep down—and that I never do. I ask her how she is doing every day! And I can see how she is doing all the time physically and emotionally; I can see it in her body language and the expressions on her face. "How are you?" I ask. "Not great" is her usual response. I am always giving her the space to feel whatever she is feeling, but I guess she needs for me to ask her, even though she wants autonomy and not have me hovering all the time.

Yesterday's awkward conversation about money was terrible: what it's being spent on, her putting me on the spot about a couple of Spiga restaurant purchases, her fear of not having enough, and her feeling the need to go back to work. I had to tell her about how much money I spent on food in the last ten days, and how I really don't have any money. A few hundred dollars in my account, and it's only the beginning of the month.

She hates the wheelchair, she hates the shower chair, and she hates the new shower sprayer; she has made that perfectly clear. She says she feels so distant from me because I don't really ask her how she is doing!! What about the fact that I am sleeping on the couch, or that there hasn't been any physical intimacy in five years! Or that maybe she doesn't know how I am feeling, because if I shared that I have felt depressed, wanting to run away, and grumpy and annoyed most of the time, it wouldn't help with the healing or comfort, so I don't share those things and maybe don't ask. This sucks big time.

Day 57
Feb 14

I finished the book *Final Gifts*. It has been very helpful, allowing me to better understand what someone is going through while in hospice and giving me some "nearing death awareness." And to try not to react to things Janet says or the tone of her voice.

Janet seems stable at this point. A routine has been created. I've been on the couch for a month. She has her protein drinks in the morning, some pretzels during the day, and a very small portion of dinner at around 4:30. In bed by 8, lights off by 9. She weighs 102 pounds, and besides her abdomen looking like she is pregnant, her bones are very pronounced. She is doing some things for herself, like getting dressed and undressed. Showering every fourth day or so. She occasionally does some dishes, but sits in her Zero Gravity Chair most of the day. She reads a little and watches TV shows. Sometimes she talks about booking tickets to go to Tim's wedding in June. Sometimes she talks about spreading her ashes. Sometimes she panics about the lack of money.

Karen is coming for a visit from February 27 to March 1. I am going to Florida to visit Lena from March 24 to 27, and Marlon is going to Maine from March 4 to 28. I woke up thinking about the mandala business and how I can get the website updated… I don't really know, but at least I was thinking about it. Suzy visits today, Gretchen tomorrow, Lois on Sunday, and Dana next week sometime. Aja, Kaelan, and Manda came last weekend, which was great. I am going to see Captain America with them on Saturday before Aja goes back to Atlanta. I might see Dagan on Sunday. I'll admit that I am feeling the financial crunch and trying not to let it overwhelm me.

Day 58
Feb 18

Routine, routine, routine. Routine is comfortable and ok. Resting in her chair, calories from the Ensure protein drink and one small meal at 4:30 seem to be enough to sustain Janet for a while. Muscle mass on her arms barely exists and is noticeable only when I put cream on her body at night. There has been some improvement in her willingness and ability to get up and make her own drinks in the morning and prepare food in the afternoon, as well as make the bed and get herself dressed. This is all such a huge improvement. It seems that the proton radiation has given her some relief. Putting cream on her belly, I can see that the swelling from the tumor under her skin has been diminished by the treatments, so the pressure is off…literally. But Janet still can't eat enough to put on the calories needed to gain some weight back. She's 101 pounds now, and I know that number bothers her. She occasionally talks about being able to drive and resume some sort of normalcy, and making arrangements for going to Tim's wedding. I never discourage these conversations, and she knows that things can go south at any point. Every morning, I wake up on the couch at 7 a.m., amazed that another day has gone by… kind of like *Groundhog Day*….

Forcing myself to write at least every few days. Today I'll see Lars at 10:30, then bring Janet to get her pump flushed at MSK in Harrison at 2:30. Then bring Kaelan my car to borrow because he got in an accident. Thank god, he and Manda are ok!

Day 59
Feb 20

Dana is visiting right now, and she brought some soup. I love that, because I wasn't sure what I was going to eat the next few days. We were at Sloan Kettering for three hours on Tuesday to get the pump flushed. So many sick people.... It's really hard to see the struggles of everyone waiting their turn for treatments.

Talking to Janet this morning about the *Final Gifts* book and how it helped me understand what she is going through. We also discussed the movie *The Room Next Door*. Tilda Swinton plays someone who is dying of cancer. I didn't like the soundtrack, but the movie was very good. Dying with dignity and the legal bullshit that goes along with it. I'm looking forward to going to Florida for a few days next week. It's so freaking cold out right now. Karen is coming for six days.

Day 60
Mar 9

Janet's dad passed away last night. No family with him. Alone in a nursing home. No "thoughts and prayers" from people who know him to guide him on his transition…drugged so it seems to everyone else that he died peacefully. Janet said she wished she had had a better relationship with him….

Janet got a six-week saline refill of her pump two days ago. They have removed the steroids, and her body is undergoing a "steroid crash." Nighttime sleep has been rough for her, and today she has been sleeping in her chair for the past four hours. I've been staying quiet, busying myself with walking, organizing cars, making breakfast, reading, and writing. I feel like my life is just about waiting…like the dead tree still standing in the woods waiting for THE moment to fall.

The other day on my morning walk, there was no wind, still pretty cold, I noticed a particular dead tree because of its cool-shaped trunk. I paused, thinking that I should take a picture of it, but I decided not to and kept walking. Thirty seconds later, I heard a pop, almost like a gunshot. I turned around to see the tree fall to the ground with a big crash. What are the chances of that happening? And if I had stopped to take a picture of it, it would have happened as I was standing next to it. Was something in a different realm trying to tell me to pay better attention? Or is there some other explanation or meaning for it?

Day 61
Mar 12

It's been a rough week for Janet. Tonight, she is throwing up for the first time since before the proton radiation treatment. Two months! She has been in so much discomfort since she had her pump flush on the 7th. Gas! Constipation, nose bleeds, and pulling out some crazy bloody membranes from her nose and throat. Her belly is now so bloated that she almost looks pregnant. Last night was the first good night sleep in a week, so I was hoping she would be feeling better today. She is barely eating anything; today, a small bowl of cereal around 2:30 and an Ensure.

Day 62
Mar 13

I'm doing ok. Witnessing Janet suffer is the hardest thing I have ever had to do…over and over again. I wish her some relief and peace. I can't imagine that the end isn't near for her. Four days away from her body shutting down a year ago, when I brought her to the hospital for a month. Yes, I am very nervous about the end and what it might look like if she can't make it to the MAID process in Vermont. I am hoping that she realizes that her "quality of life" is really pretty bad, with not much improvement likely in the future…. I guess she is trying to make it to Tim's wedding in June, but how sick will she be by then? She is making whimpering sounds all the time now, from extreme discomfort, I guess.

These are the symptoms Janet's experiencing now:

   * shortness of breath

   * extreme discomfort around the pump area

   * sharp discomfort when burping, hiccupping, or moving

   * bloody noses

   * hemorrhoids

   * constipation

   * lots of gas

   * abdomen swollen and tight

   * yellow eyes

Day 63
Mar 14

Now that the weather has been a bit warmer, I've been walking the path two times a day.

8:30 p.m.: Times like tonight, when Janet is suffering gas pain and in the bathroom for 45 minutes spitting up blood and hacking…she has lost so much blood over the past few days. I question…. When will this end? Sometimes it feels like it's too hard to witness her suffering. Too bad, because it's coming off a pretty good visit with Remony and Phyllida for over three hours earlier today. First time, Janet was smiling in weeks, if not months. But after they left, she came crashing down. She said that, besides me and Marlon, they were her favorite people, and that's why she perked up for so long.

Day 64
Mar 15

Another day.... I'll blink and it'll be bedtime, that's how it has been lately...day after day. Janet was so wiped out last night that I had to undress her and dress her for bed. I'm doing my best to sense when to assist her and when to let her do the simple things, like helping her dress or get her Ensure in the morning, or holding her arm when she goes from her chair to the bathroom and back. She did take a shower by herself yesterday, but when she came out of the bathroom, she could barely stand. I wonder each day: Will this be her last? But then I realize that this could go on for a while yet. She is still getting out of bed and doing some things for herself. But she isn't getting much nutrition, so isn't it just a matter of time?

Day 65
Mar 16

A year ago tonight, Janet had her near-death experience!

Day 66
Mar 17

10 a.m., and Janet is still not awake yet. Twelve hours asleep. I lie down with her every night for a couple of hours and fall asleep myself. When I wake up, I go and sleep in the other room on the couch so my tossing and turning doesn't keep her up.

The Vermont trip to Grace Cottage Hospital for the first doctor visit about MAID is on Thursday. Incredible because a few months ago, I thought no way Janet would make it this far. I might have to take her for an X-ray today because her belly is so bloated and extended. Lots of blood coming out of her today, and she is looking so ill. Moaning in the bathroom and coughing up so much blood and pulling out strings of blood from her nose—she calls them "blood worms." I think it's probably the lining of her stomach or something.

Day 67
Mar 18

Coughing and blowing out blood all night. I can't imagine enduring that for so long. My night of waking up every time she blew her nose or coughed reminded me of the first year having twins, when I didn't get any sleep. If I got an hour at a time, I was lucky. It sucks and can only go on for so long before everything starts falling apart. Lois and Ken are supposed to come for a visit today, but maybe they shouldn't, or if they do, just come and not talk, just sit.

Day 68
Mar 20

At the hospital in White Plains with Janet because of possible liver failure. It's been a rough few days of constant nose bleeding and coughing up blood clots. Again at the hospital, and again telling the story of what Janet has gone through these past few weeks, over and over to all the doctors and nurses. It is the first day of spring. Janet is dying. We've been in the hospital since Tuesday. The bleeding won't stop coming out of her nose and throat. Her liver is failing, and this is what it looks like. She is so weak and frail at this point.

Karen came from Atlanta halfway through the day and took over bedside. After a bit of a scramble, Karen was able to find and arrange for home hospice care. Karl and Tim are on their way to the hospital, probably to see Janet for the last time. I'm not sure if Janet fully understands; her mind seems a bit foggy. It seems that her nose bleeding has stopped. I was so nervous about bringing her home, bleeding the way she was.

Every time I have to share what is going on with Janet, with Suzy and Dana, I have an overwhelming sense of sadness. Her abilities are deteriorating. She talks in whispers and can't move her body very well. This is day number 3 without any nourishment. I came home, made the bed, and took a nap. They did two transfusions, gave her fluids, antibiotics, a CT scan, and did blood tests. Her skin got a little better. But the blood wouldn't stop coming out.

Poor Janet, she is so uncomfortable. I am nervous about bringing her home. Hospice is necessary. Marlon flies home from Maine tomorrow. I hope Janet makes it to then. I'll shower and then head back to the hospital. I am so nervous…about the details and have been for months.

Day 69
Mar 21

2:45 pm: Janet is on her way home from the hospital right now in an ambulance. I've prepped the house. A hospital bed set up in the bedroom. Hospice meds have arrived; the nurse will be here after Janet is settled. I went for a quick walk, and every time I thought of Janet's friends saying goodbye to her, the tears started flowing. Marlon should be home from Maine in an hour or so. And people want to visit. Aunt Janet, Suzy, Dana. So far, we have about 28 birthday cards for her.

Thank god, Janet stopped bleeding once she stopped taking the blood thinner meds. I am so relieved about that. I have been very nervous about it. I still am, but not as much. I have been watching Janet deteriorate for such a long time. Acceptance, compassion, and Love! What am I going to do? Once Janet is gone? Busy myself…with cleaning, organizing, maybe painting? I am pretty fucking tired. Kaelan has been visiting me. I am so lucky to have him in my life and relatively close by.

Day 70
Mar 24

It's been a rough couple of days since we have been home from the hospital. The roller coaster ride continues. I have been very upset about what feels like disrespect from Janet's family and being in our tiny little house. So many people in a small space, with the voice volume too high. I ended up getting upset and telling them all that it is unacceptable! Today was a bit better, but then Aunt Janet and Lois brought four bottles of wine. My heart rate went through the roof—I could feel my heart thumping in my chest and limbs, and I said that they cannot bring them in here. Drawing boundary lines is not easy and not my favorite thing to do. So, I went out to Dunkin' and sat in my car eating donuts while they visited with Janet for an hour and a half. When I came home, I had a quiet time with Janet and Marlon. Karen went out to dinner with them all, so she got a break from the house as well. Dana visited for 45 minutes, and Suzy visited for an hour. Janet was awake for nine-plus hours! She ate a little food.

Overall, she is bloated in her ankles, legs, hips, and especially her abdomen. Her skin feels so tight to the touch. Tonight, she walked to the bathroom and bedroom from her chair without assistance. She is having a hard time breathing, so tomorrow she will start with the oxygen. Today was an up day on the roller coaster ride. Sometimes it's up and down from hour to hour. This is all really fucking hard!!! Today I really wanted to abandon ship and leave this all behind. Again, tomorrow will come and go.... I love you Janet…good night. I am doing my best.

Day 71
Mar 26

Long Day! Every night, helping Janet to bed is difficult in different ways. Lying in her hospital bed, she looks like she could die tonight. I needed to help her get from the chair to the bathroom and then to the bedroom. It took 15 minutes for her to gather the strength to get out of the chair. No muscle strength in her abdomen, and her feet, ankles, knees, legs, and hips are so swollen. She tried a few bites of dinner, but I am afraid it will cause gas and give her "discomfort."

The social worker came, so now we can set up the crematorium details, which we are all on board with. Then, the RN and PT nurses came. All good support. I am not as nervous now that things are in place. It still is an up-and-down feeling as the day goes on. I can't imagine that Janet's small body, as swollen as it is, can go on for very much longer. But she never ceases to amaze me every single day. I cannot assume anything.

Day 72
Mar 26

Some depression started creeping into me today. I feel bad
that I want it to end sooner rather than later; obviously, it will
end whenever it is Janet's "time." So why do I feel depressed at
times? I have had five and a half years of processing the end and
what it might be like after she dies, and I am all by myself.
I love her so much, and I'm not sure how it will be for me
without having to take care of her. Will it be loneliness or feel
like a relief? What task will I have to do? What will my purpose
be? There are so many questions as I walk alone and around
the property, while I am driving my car...as I lay in bed trying
to get to sleep. I really am just "rolling with it." She looks so
sick to me. The color of her skin, her swollen lower half, and
her bony arms, shoulders, and wrists. The mystery of when and
what the end will look like for her. The crematorium is set up
and in place now at Nutmeg State Crematorium in Stamford,
again thanks to Karen. The two things I was bugging out about
back in November, five months ago, were Hospice and the
Crematorium! So that is a bit of a relief. I am really tired and
burnt out... doing my best...Acceptance, compassion, Love!

Day 73
Mar 27

Acceptance, Compassion, and Love.

I now realize that I have been grieving the loss of Janet and my relationship with her for the past seven years. From the time she was experiencing the pain from the nerve sheath tumor…our relationship has never been the same as before. We have had some moments of beauty, but I have had a sense of loss since then. Now I am having moments of grief because I am losing a companion to this dreadful, long, terminal illness of cancer. We may be down to the last days and weeks, but I am feeling like there will be more of a sense of relief than grief. Relief that she and I won't have to endure the struggle anymore, and a sense of grief for the sadness that Janet's light won't be right next to me anymore, with her sense of humor and her beautiful face.

Today, Janet slept until noon. I helped her to her chair, she was bathed by nurse Catherine at 3 slept on the couch from 4 to 7:30, ate a little quiche, watched the most recent episode of *The Pitt*, and was in bed by 9:30. Awake for a total of 6 hours. Tomorrow, no visitors.

Day 74
Mar 28

Not much to say about today. Another day, Janet slept until noon. I played my guitar for her until she got into her chair. We tried taking a nap together on the couch. I liked that she wanted to do that with me. Lois bought Chinese food for dinner. Janet ate a little noodles and spinach. I walked. My breathing has been bad, so I have been using my inhaler again.

Tomorrow, Janet turns 60! Incredible that she has made it to this milestone. She is bloated from her abdomen down and super skinny in her chest and arms. Her face is looking very sick to me, but she keeps plugging along, out of breath and unable to dress and undress herself, even if it is just her pajamas and socks. I keep expecting her to maybe not want to get up out of bed or not want to eat... but she keeps going.... How....? And why?

Day 75
Mar 29

SHE MADE IT TO HER BIRTHDAY...60!!!

I am amazed.

Happy birthday, Janet... I don't know what else to say....

Day 76
Mar 30

After Janet endured the birthday dinner and cake and cards, we finally got her to bed between 9:30 and 10. I sat with her holding her hand, and she said to me with her eyes closed, "They aren't going to let me go."

Me: "Who aren't going to let you go?"

A long silence… "My mom and Marlon."

Me: "We are all ready to let you go…we have all talked about it…your mom is ready to let you go… Marlon is ready to let you go…Karen is ready to let you go…I am ready to let you go… whenever you are ready to let go…. Let go…. There are beautiful souls on the other side waiting for you…. Amy Lee is waiting for you with all her love."

And as I was saying this, the most beautiful smile came over her face and stayed there for five minutes. I held her hand and listened to her very slow and shallow breath for another half hour before I fell asleep. I thought maybe this is her last breath. I woke up at 1 a.m. to hear her breathing. For the rest of the night, she fidgeted, tossed, coughed, and…kept breathing. I really thought that was going to be it…. She said she doesn't want to get out of bed anymore. I lay awake all night… listening…for her last breath.

Day 77
Apr 2

Finally, a decent night's sleep. Karen went back to Atlanta
yesterday. And Claudia, the home health aide, came and bathed
Janet, who was awake and in her chair most of the day.
Last night was the second night Janet took the morphine meds,
which definitely helped her sleep and also helped me sleep.
I think I've accepted that this is the "long haul." I had to help
Janet up from a sitting position twice because the muscles in
her swollen abdomen were too weak. Then she used the walker to
get from the chair to the bathroom and bedroom.
Yesterday, she had two bites of a tuna sandwich, which created
intense gas discomfort.

Because of the ups and downs of Janet's energy and her cognitive
abilities going in and out, we have all come to peace with the
eventual outcome. Maybe that is the healthy process and part
of why she is still hanging on to life. We have done all the right
things, from hospice care to family and friends visiting, to foods
or no foods, to meds and no meds, as well as being present and
looking ahead. We've allowed space and time for her to make
her own willful decisions regarding all of the above. It's all up to
Janet. This is as dignified as it can be without going to Vermont
for the MAID process.

I've been thinking about what I am going to say at Janet's
memorial as I walk the path every day. I guess I should start
writing some notes so that I'll remember what I want to say,
because right now my mind is a BLANK.

Day 78
Apr 3

What a trip this is! This morning, Marlon and I held Janet's
hands while she was having a nightmare. She has been in and out
of sleep all day today, and right now she is looking at her phone.
She hasn't had a sip of water since 7:30 last night and no food at
all since 4:40 the day before. She didn't want the nurse to bathe
her today, saying she just wanted to stay in bed and have it quiet.
As I watched her sleeping all morning, her breath was slow and
sporadic to the point where I'm thinking…today has got to be
the day. And then she wakes up and looks at her phone for
a while, and goes back to sleep. Now she wants her pill…that she
didn't take yesterday. And she wants to get in her chair and have
some Ensure…??? One minute near death, the next… keeping
going. She made a comment about noisy visitors she didn't want,
and I BUGGED OUT! I went and met Kaelan while he was on
his dinner break, while on set in Purchase, New York; then got
a burger and fries, and feeling very guilty, went to the movies.
I kissed Janet good night and told her I loved her. Marlon took
care of her while I was out…. It sounded very hard for her.
It's a flip-flop for me as well. One day, I accept that we are in it
for the long haul, the next I am resentful as fuck. She is the one
dying! Why can't I just be loving and compassionate always?
I feel terrible about the way I feel…. FUUUUCK!!!

Day 79
Apr 4

Janet needed to go to the bathroom at 11 p.m. and again at 6:30 a.m.—a little poop both times. When I got her back into bed, she said she was uncomfortable. So, I said, "I think the morphine could help with that. It has helped you for the past three nights." But she argued that she only took it two times…two times at night and once during the day, trying to prove me wrong all the way to the end. It's very hard not to take these things personally, even when she is on her "deathbed." What kind of cosmic joke is this? Janet hanging on and making me suffer right along with her for as long as possible? Acceptance, compassion, love…. I feel like my abilities are fading.

Day 80
Apr 6

Today was a quiet day. No visitors, Marlon went and spent most of the day with their dad. It was drizzly and grey all day, and I didn't feel like opening the curtains. I sat near Janet for a good portion of the day in the bedroom, reading. She woke up at 5:30 p.m. and was surprised at the time. And a bit confused and funny. She said that she was dreaming of dogs, and when she opened her eyes, thought I was a poodle sitting on the chair. I watched her sleep in and out of dream state and with a heavier breath than the previous very light breathing of the past few weeks.

Today is 17 days since we brought her home from the hospital! And each day, I have imagined it being her last day. In today's quietness, I really worked on letting go of any expectations around when she will pass and how it will come to be. Funny Janet saying, "5:30 and a poodle" and "Wisdom from the waiting room."

Day 81
Apr 7

Today I don't expect Janet will pass. She might, but probably won't, so I expect that she will sleep until she wakes up, say some things, want to get into her chair for a while, then get back into bed. This is where we are right now…. Accept it…no projections or how it should be or what should be happening. Just be here. We all talked for a little while last night about how nice it was to have the house quiet and the rest she needs and wants, even if it is to sleep for 24 hours. She wants the nurses to come less often, so we are telling hospice to come on Wednesday instead of today. Janet is still declining and getting weaker by the day. I saw that she didn't have the strength to cut up a small piece of hamburger last night, so I cut it into small bites for her. I think she appreciated that. We have to help her stand up from a sitting position in the chair, when she gets off the toilet, and when she is getting out of bed. I think that is why my back hurts today. She wanted a double dose of morphine last night, and I noticed a bit more movement in the middle of the night than the night before.

Last night she said some funny things about being buried with her earrings on, and being in death's waiting room, and to keep checking her breathing if she sleeps all day. I am sorry I wasn't able to record her sense of humor. There really is no making sense of all this. It is my job as a compassionate human to allow space for Janet's process without the emotional baggage of control, resentment, ego, and expectation. And to fully accept her transition, no matter how long it may be, with compassion and love.

Day 82
Apr 8

Amy would've been 28 today! If there is any kind of cosmic connection, I sure wish Amy would help Janet on her way. She is looking so cancer-ill, with barely enough strength to open her eyes and sit on the toilet. Today I write as I sit bedside with her, watching her facial expressions and the blanket rising and falling as she sleeps.... So much sleep. I keep thinking and questioning, "Is that her last breath?"

It's been weeks of this uncertainty. Marlon and I discussed this morning how everything will change drastically when she passes. Although I have come to a place of acceptance around her passing, until I am in a world without Janet, I won't really know what it is going to be like.

Health aide coming at 2.... It's a little after noon, and the chimes are chiming. People still text and ask how Janet is doing...not sure how to respond. I really don't want to have to explain what is going on.... She is dying. Please wait for the message that she has passed and stop asking me how she is doing!

Day 83
Apr 9

Rough night…. I helped Janet up to go to the bathroom at 11:30. At 1:30, she was moaning and groaning in pain. At 2, she finally agreed to two single doses of morphine as suggested by the Saturday nurse, and 40 minutes later, she wanted another dose, saying that she was in so much pain that she wanted to die. This morning, she said she is alright, in and out of sleep. I notice some changes in her face. When her eyelids are closed, they are a lot darker brown than usual. When she opens them, her eyes seem to roll up in her head before she can focus. And there are now small skin creases on either side of the corners of her mouth that I didn't notice yesterday. Janet said she thought she was having a heart attack in the night around 2:30 a.m.

Every day as I sit bedside with her in the mornings, I listen to her deep breathing with exceptionally long pauses and wonder if there is any reasoning for the suffering—not only of Janet but anyone who is going through the physical and psychological struggles of being human. Whether it is a terminal illness or something else…war and torture, oppression from others, drugs. Some say it is our soul or spirit's journey…. I am questioning that big time. Of course, I would like to believe that the light of love after we are here as beings in this physical realm is real, but is the suffering so necessary? I do realize that the cancer cells are just another organism trying to survive, eating away at its host until there is nothing left. It's a terrible thing, no one should have to endure it…. Like the prison camps, it's a plague on humans… innocents being destroyed by a dreadful force.

Day 84
Apr 10

Another rough night…. Janet needed to get up out of bed in a hurry after sleeping deeply for almost a full 24 hours, to get to the toilet because a suppository that the nurse gave her to help her poop was taking effect. She had explosive diarrhea and thought she had soiled the bed; thankfully, she didn't. I got her back in bed, and she was very confused about time and when the nurse and Natalie had come 12 hours earlier. Before I helped her go to the bathroom, she had fidgeted with her eyes and nose for an hour or so, so I wasn't getting any sleep—just lying there listening to her breath and the rustling of the covers. After she got back into bed, she said she wasn't in any pain and didn't want any more of the morphine we hadn't given to her at "bedtime." Because she was in a deep sleep already, I didn't want to wake her up. I explained what the nurse had said about staying on top of the pain, but Janet didn't want it unless she couldn't get back to sleep.

Now it's noon. She needed to poop again and then wanted to get in her chair. So now we are listening to Pat Metheny. She is so small, still occasionally sipping on water, occasionally looking off into the distance, obviously somewhere else in her mind's eye. She seems confused with everything we are saying, she wasn't sure what Sonic ice was…in and out of sleep. I hold her cold hand, twitching now and again. We canceled nurse Claudia, who was supposed to bathe her today, and put her off till next week, if next week comes. We told Lois to come tomorrow so we could have another quiet day.

Day 85
Apr 11

Another day arrives, and Janet is still alive. Every time I assume or expect things to be a certain way, I am wrong. After sitting in the chair for a few hours yesterday, she asked to get on the bed where she lay awake looking out the window with the oxygen going in her nose. She had a couple of bites of ice cream and immediately threw up. She has pooped three times since the nurse was here two days ago and gave her the suppository.

Janet wanted the morphine last night when we went to bed at 8:30, and we all had a restful night. For me, I think it was a combination of her not rustling the covers and my acceptance that she probably wasn't going to die tonight, so I didn't have to be on high alert. And her breathing was so quiet that I couldn't hear it anyway. I slept for 10 hours. Janet opened her eyes when I got up and said Hello…. But now she is back in a deep sleep. It's amazing how long she has lasted with very little nutrition. It's been 64 hours since she had her last two bites of a chicken nugget at Amy's birthday dinner, and it was a couple of days before that she had a couple of bites of something? Maybe a burger. Nurse Erik is coming today from 11 to 1:30, and Lois is coming around noon. I'll step out when she arrives. It's best for everyone. I am hoping Janet won't feel the need to get out of bed.

Day 86
Apr 12

Here I am again, sitting at the foot of the bed quietly reading and listening and watching. Waiting… expecting that last breath. Unfortunately, I play a numbers game. How many hours since Janet ate anything? At this moment, it's been 87 hours! 13 hours since she had a sip of water! How many seconds of pauses between breaths? Sometimes 15 seconds! Her chimes are chiming, and it's a cold 39 degrees out and raining—a really fucking gloomy day.

I walked down the driveway before having coffee this morning because I had to get out of the house. I watched a beautiful Robin sitting on the wall for a while, wondering about the cosmic connection…if there is one? At times, I feel so honored that I am experiencing this transition with Janet and able to help her as her body deteriorates, when she can't hold her toothbrush and can't get up by herself. Watching her as she struggles to open her eyes. Seeing her hands shake as she touches the itch on her face. At other times, I feel so helpless because I want the end to be a certain way, to feel certain things, to have some sort of divine cosmic connection with her as she transitions. What is really going on here? Can she make some conscious decisions? Why is she still suffering? It looks like suffering…or is that just how I am interpreting it? Will we have more moments of conversation? Or is she going into a transition coma? Will there be a sudden body movement or realization when death comes, or will she just stop breathing? Will she pass with a realization that she is waking up from a dream that she created with her life in this world and be set free from the bounds of this physical realm?

Maybe post this on Facebook when she passes:

It is with a broken heart that I share with you the passing of my beloved Janet Schuman. A broken heart because she was a shining light who not only chose to share her life with me these past 16 years, but also because her loving presence will be missed by everyone whose lives she touched in her 60 years on this planet. A relief because living with cancer these past five and a half years has been the most difficult time of our lives, and she is now at peace. Janet's will and determination to LIVE with cancer have been beautiful and challenging at the same time. Challenging to see her suffer the pain and recovery from all the surgeries and sickness, and from the 59 rounds of chemo. And yet, how she recovered from those surgeries and rebounded after her chemo were a beautiful thing to witness. She loved her family, friends, and her yoga community so much so that, as soon as she was able, she would get right back to what she enjoyed most...making sure others were comfortable. There will be a memorial service at the Yoga Loft at the Bedford Post Inn, where we will be honoring Janet's life in the place she made special for so many. Please bring any pictures or stories to share with friends and family.

Day 87
Apr 13

I woke up in a total funk today! I didn't want to see anyone or respond to anyone. I turned off my phone at 6 a.m. and didn't get out of bed till 10:30. In and out of sleep, waking up very aware of Janet's breathing going silent for long periods of time… and then the recovery breath or her itching her face. I thought, "She is still breathing, she is still breathing, she is still breathing." It should be a song or a poem. So here we are, another day. Janet is way more confused today, saying things like, "Did you make dinner reservations?" or "There is a bug under the desk." She takes long and loud sighs now and then…a big release of stuck energy, I suppose.

Marlon has gone to the YMCA to work out until Natalie comes to work on Janet's feet at 2. I need to get out as well. I'll probably go to another movie. Lois has been put off till tomorrow…I am sure she is feeling like we are putting her off.

Day 88
Apr 14

Finally, a sunny day… amazing what a difference the sun makes. Yesterday evening, after Marlon and I ate pizza for dinner, Janet wanted to go to the bathroom and then get into her chair from her bed. That is getting harder and harder because of how weak she has become, especially her legs and knees. She wanted to eat two crackers. After being confused about the final episodes of The Pitt, which she had already seen and realized it 15 minutes in, we ended up watching two episodes of The Diplomat instead. She was mixing up the characters and the fact that we had already seen all of The Diplomat episodes as well. And then it was such a struggle to get her back into bed. Then she was being so cute and expressing her gratitude to Marlon and me for taking such good care of her, and that she wouldn't know what to do without us!!! This is day 6 without any food, yet right now she is constantly trying to clear her throat of the blood goo that she pushes out. Where is it all coming from? It's a sound that I definitely won't miss when this is all over.

9:30 p.m.…. I can't sleep after lying next to her for four hours, listening and thinking and listening and thinking. The shit that is swirling around in my head.…

Earlier today, I completely bugged out when Lois was here. I told Marlon that I was done, I'm out!!! And I am not coming back. I took money out of my drawer with the intention of not coming back…RUNNING! Lois nonchalantly talked to Janet about Ken bringing sandwiches for lunch, so Janet felt like she should eat something because everyone else would be eating something…A TURKEY SANDWICH!!! She doesn't eat gluten and doesn't like turkey! I literally threw my hands up and said, "GO AHEAD. GIVE HER A FUCKING SANDWICH!!!" And this was after I explained to Lois why I thought giving and offering Janet food at this point was probably a bad idea because food was causing her so much gas pain. "You will have to deal with getting her to the bathroom, because I am so outta here!" They gave her the sandwich anyway. I was so upset that I stormed out with my cash in hand, intending to run and not look back. I decided to go into town to the bank. As I sat outside the bank, I called Aja. He talked me down off the ledge. I was a sobbing mess…. I went to the bank, got gas, and contemplated which direction I should go. Aja said that I would regret it if I ran, and that I would have a harder time pulling my life together after this all passes. He is probably right… It's going to be really hard anyway… I decided to hang out in my car at Waveny Park. Dagan sent me a *New York Times* article about Phish, I listened to the Dune soundtrack, got a text from Manda and Kaelan saying that I can come and live with them. I got a large coffee and a half dozen donuts and sat for a few hours.

I came home, didn't say shit, took a shower, got into bed, and listened to her breathing. I thought about how fucked up things have been for a very long time. It's been a month of listening for the last breath. Before that, it was, and still is, that she is in so much discomfort leading up to and through the proton radiation. Before that, it was the Thanksgiving to Christmas decline. Before that, it was the river cruise in Europe. Before that it was six rounds and three months of chemo. Before that, it was recovery from last year's near-death experience. Before that, it was recovery from surgery when the pump was installed. Before that, it was six months of chemo…. Oh, was there any joy in our relationship? Right now, I am not remembering any. And my financial situation is feeling so fucked up with taxes, and the living situation here….

It feels very similar to 16 years ago when I ran from my ex-wife and Vermont…. That was bad! This is just as bad. But I know I have to stick it out and do the right thing this time. I am really not seeing a clear way through the financial piece. In Vermont, I also went back the day I bugged out, but I didn't last the night…. I thought I was hearing the beginning of the death rattle in Janet when I was lying in bed next to her earlier… This all sucks so bad!!! Traumatized again. Interesting how all three kids stepped up and supported me today.

Day 89
Apr 15

When I finally did go to bed last night, I slept ok. Got up at 6 a.m. and went for a slow walk. Janet was awake when I got back and said it felt like a week had passed since she had been awake. She said she dreamt of needing to be in Atlanta because something had happened to Tim. He was ok, but we needed to be there. Another part of her dream was that she was late to get on a plane to go to a dance trip with college friends, whom she didn't recognize, and that she was all wet… Then she jumped out the window of the plane with skis on. Then she needed to go to the bathroom. Marlon helped. Then she wanted to get into her chair, so we helped her into the wheelchair and brought her into the living room to her chair. As she sat there, she said that she wished she had made it to Vermont for the MAID process. I apologized for not making that happen for her; she missed it by one day, being so sick in the hospital. I oversimplified things and said, "That MAID would've been a choice… you still have that choice right now to be done with all of this." Obviously, it's not that easy. Janet said she is sorry that this is making me mad. I said it's not, that I just wanted to see some relief for her. She said that maybe she could sleep in her chair tonight? Ok.

Day 90
Apr 16

Janet's liver failure is turning out to be a way longer process than anyone could've imagined. I guess it's been failing for many months, but I thought the endgame would go faster. Still wondering what this is all teaching me and how I am going to move on when Janet's life is over.... Does anyone ever feel healed from the trauma they experience? Because this is some serious trauma...the long, drawn-out kind. I wonder how Janet would be handling this if I were dying and she had to take care of me...unable to walk or move from side to side, unable to bathe or eat or get up and down off the toilet. Would she be by my side most of the time, like I am right now? Reading and writing next to her as she goes in and out of sleep at 8 a.m., day after day, trying to accommodate anything she wants or needs. Erik the nurse comes at noon today.... And so it goes.

Day 91
Apr 18

Janet says, "I think people need their own personal coffee tables," and then she looks at Moo the stuffed highland cow and says, "You have no idea what we are talking about, do you?" The confusion of what goes on in her mind is sometimes comical. It's hard to make sense of her train of thought.... She quotes my mom out of the blue. "Your mom would say, 'Get on with it !'" True, that is exactly what my mom would say.

10:30 p.m.: rough getting Janet into bed tonight. She was very frustrated at me and herself for not being able to communicate what she wanted done with the sheets, comforter, and pillows. And all of a sudden, she didn't realize that for the past month, she had a sheet between her and the comforter and kept wanting me to put the sheet inside the comforter. I tried to explain, but she was getting more frustrated and insistent, so I made it look like I was rearranging things and then covered her the way I have been doing: propped her up on one side and a pillow between her legs. Gave her the meds, tucked her in, kissed her a few times, and told her I love her. Good night, Janet Schuman from high school, sleep well. I could tell she was very sad tonight. She said she feels lonely all the time. I imagine feeling confused and disabled feels really bad in so many ways. I really wasn't expecting her to lose her cognitive function and short-term memory. And that seems to be happening.

Day 92
Apr 19

It is supposed to be sunny and 83 today. Sitting with Janet and Marlon this morning, bedside, quiet, just all sitting together. Janet asks: "Matthew, did you just turn out the light?" You have to wonder what is going on in that head of hers and the neuron connections, and what is working and what isn't. The Phish tour started last night in Seattle. Maybe I'll be able to go to some shows this summer. I got my new walking stick, hell yeah!
She says, "I see a duck sitting on the wall," and, "I don't want to put the dog at the top of the castle and don't look back."
It's impossible to remember and stay on top of all the things Janet is saying.

Wow, we managed to get Janet outside for a couple of hours to-day in the wheelchair to sit in the sun and feel the breeze. It was good for all of us! Lois came to visit, and I went out. Car wash, Waveny Park, long talk with Karen on the phone with updates. Janet had some mashed potatoes for dinner, three bites, and then threw up when we went to bed. Earlier in the day, she threw up a brown goop of, flaky consistency, which was probably the two bites of steak she tried the night before.... The day before that, she threw up a fruit smoothie while Lois was visiting.

Day 93
Apr 20

We both slept well despite the crazy wind blowing the wind chimes all night long. Going into week five of hospice care! Can I appreciate being able to see Janet every morning and still take care of her? Seeing her face, enjoying her silly comments, being able to hug her as I pick her up from bed, chair, and toilet. I get to kiss the side of her face every time, lucky me!

More throwing up around 10 while in the chair, after she tried a piece of pear. We got her outside again at 11 and took some wonderful pictures. Ken and Lois visited half an hour for Easter. A small amount of Indian food at dinner time, maybe four small bites. The pills she is taking to reduce the water retention in her lower half seem to be helping; her feet and ankles aren't as swollen as much by the evening.

Day 94
Apr 21

Janet threw up three times today. At 7:15 am on the toilet, when Willa came for a visit at noon, and getting ready for bed. Spinach she had at dinner last night. Tomorrow, nurses Claudia and Erik are coming at the same time. Good visit with Dana and Willa, and a FaceTime with Karen.

Janet is really bored.... Me too with the routine of sitting. I can't imagine what it's like to be Janet. Poor Janet, I feel so bad for her.

Day 95
Apr 22

Janet got up at 9:30, and we got her outside right away. It was a beautiful morning. Back in the chair by 10:45, and throwing up. Karen booked a flight to come back on April 30. I am happy about that. I might go to Vermont for the May Day celebration on top of Putney Mountain with Dagan. Erik came at 12:15. We played drums for 15 minutes before having a very emotional and intense conversation. Sometimes it felt like the conversation kept going in circles.

Sometimes it's hard to know if it's Janet's slowing cognition that has her spinning on about the medication. And then, the throwing up, the medication again, anti-nausea meds, and more hovering. Nurse Claudia bathed her at 1:30. She lay on the couch until 6:45 with her feet up. She threw up a lot of blood today. Got back in the chair, had a couple of bites of popcorn. We sat just holding hands for quite a while before the prepping for bed routine—toilet, teeth, hands, bed, cream on back and legs. I gave her a suppository tonight because she hasn't pooped in a while. Gave her the morphine, placed her pillows, and tucked her in. She says her spine feels sore. Her body has become so misshapen, swollen in places and skin and bones in others. I love her so much, I want her to have some comfort and peace. Good night, Janet Schuman from high school, I love you. Take me with you into your dreams....

Another day done....

Day 96
Apr 23

12:45 a.m., rushing to get Janet out of bed and to the toilet to have an extremely painful diarrhea poop. The suppository worked really fast this time. Her tummy has been gurgling and grumbling for days. This morning, she didn't wake up when I got out of bed, so I sat having my coffee outside in the beautiful, warm morning sunshine. Suzy is coming over for a visit at 2:30, and Chris is coming tonight at 8 p.m.

Day 97
Apr 24

Good visit with Chris last night. Good for all of us. Janet was very coherent and clear. He told her that even though she feels ok at the moment and wants to get "better," her body, her liver, is going in the other direction, and we are all doing what we can to help her be comfortable. But instead of the process going on and on and getting more and more difficult, we should plan for her death to be what and how she wants it to be.

Yesterday was very hard. After a beautiful car ride to the water in Darien, it was so hard getting Janet out of the car when we got back. She wanted to lie down on a cushion on the patio in the sun. But trying to get her up and back into the house by myself—picking her up from the ground and trying to get her up the two steps and through the kitchen door—was so painful for her. We were both crying. Her skin is getting more sensitive, especially on either side of her chest, around her back. I got her inside, but I never want to do that again. Suzy came for a visit just as I got her back in the house and stayed for an hour. Then I went out for dinner by myself. Chris helped us get Janet back into bed, and she didn't want to try to go to the bathroom.

Today, Lois visits, and I have a 4 p.m. appointment at Anne's Place in Danbury to talk about support. Janet had a few bites of white rice, but she threw up five times today. At the edge of the bed, on the toilet, in her chair, lying on the couch, and on the toilet again, getting ready for bed.

Day 98
Apr 25

Janet didn't eat any food yesterday, a few bites…. Scratch that! She ate a little rice, then barfed. The day before, a few beans, then barfed, and before that, a couple of pieces of popcorn, then barfed. Basically, she is being sustained by drinking water. Waking up she said, "Finally my feet don't hurt." Were they hurting? "Yeah, about a month ago, they really hurt."

She woke up early today, 6:30, 7:00. Toilet—barf, from 9:30 outside til noon. Nurse Karyn came at 12:40 and ordered some ear patches to maybe help with the vomiting. Today, Janet threw up seven times. One of those times, it looked like the bloody fleshy lining of the stomach. She says she feels so sick when she talks to me, but says she feels "ok" to the nurse. She says she remembers a dream from a few days ago. It was a few days before her death day, and she asked Kaelan and Aja to take care of the details for her memorial, but for some reason, they couldn't, so she took care of it after she died."

Tonight, she says she sometimes sees more than just me and Marlon in the room. So, we asked if it was other people or a couple more Marlons and Matthews? She said it was more of us??? Multiple Matthews and Marlons….

Tomorrow, Natasha comes to visit, and Phillipe and David come to drum at 4! I am going to meet Dana at 10:15. Get popsicles from the farmers market and go to the post office.

Day 99
Apr 26

2 pm. Sitting bedside with Janet. She is not present and continually talks what seems to be nonsense to someone I can't see or feel. She keeps using her hands like she is using a cell phone. And making movements like she is eating something and reaching for something. I'll try to write down what she is saying as she says it.

[She isn't really aware that I am right next to her. Her eyes are wide open, occasionally reaching for something or someone, occasionally shrugging her shoulders, and constantly straightening out tissues that she keeps pulling from the tissue box and hoarding under the blanket. Sometimes it's hard to hear her speaking so softly.]

"Anyway…yea…maybe ummmm…no, ok. I am voil that I am in. They are not doing it any longer, so we will see, or the relationship with my day or something like that…. Got you… and then can't be 70 or something…and…yes…. I said one of the things I'm planning. Please let's…did they have a good time, another time… all right then…ok….ok…and so take a break… different…then….yeah, was that this discussion…yes, I am starting to…yes…yes, but I'm not really closer to the clock…. Do you want to get up? It's funny how there is hundreds of…. I'm doing what I wanted to do…. Then that's my chicken… oatmilk, just one of those ummmm…it's just…yeah pardon? They had me see the outfit. I feel like an orange…not right here…. Radio's ok, I'll do that, it all works out…yes…I don't mean… what's that? (*reaching out to touch something or someone*) And actually I…Kay, ok…all right then. I am, but you know how that goes. You can't do that… the cream…write a note to your…. Kite, I just want to go up…the best way expected. I should do the printing…this day has and these…it's just like (*a grabbing motion in front of her*) yeah, and my dear…alright. I think that…get it… yeah (*agreeing with someone and nodding her head*). My mom versus…which would probably cause deer eyes….. yeah, wow, I did know to keep up with…. Thank you… ok…I am ok…you're ok… yeah, and even in the buffet section… yeah…(*looking straight at me*) could secret and my apply? I'll have a little rice from that…what?... sure…ok…ok… rest…you can trim…you never like torrential (*picks up the glass of water by the bed and lets go of it on the bed*). Before I go back…I'm just…. What do we need…it's not great…let us know, I'll…I'll get the milk, they have a canvas bag…word…come back in an hour or so…which one? You come first.

This conversation with whoever was with her went on for about an hour and a half.

Day 100
Apr 27

I'm not sure how to explain how I feel about the turn Janet has taken. The nurse came yesterday after I called hospice in a bit of a panic about this change in Janet, and insisted that the ear patch to help her with the vomiting was causing this hallucinatory state. So the nurse took it off and said it may take some time for these possible side effects to wear off. She also put a catheter in Janet, so she doesn't have to get out of bed every time she has the urge to pee.

After a long day of Janet not being Janet and a struggle to get her to the toilet to do an imaginary poop, we gave her Lorazepam and morphine, and it took an hour and a half for her to stop her rapid-fire talking and fall asleep around 9:30. Then at 5:15 a.m. she woke up and started talking again immediately. I want the old Janet back, please.

She can't seem to suck on a straw anymore, so now I am giving her drops of water with a syringe. This could also be the stage she is in before going into the sleep coma that I have been expecting, but maybe it will change.... I don't like it because she isn't answering basic questions like, How are you? or Are you thirsty?, so we have to guess if she is comfortable. I wish we hadn't given her the anti-vomit ear patch…but she did agree to it when she was cognitive.

Day 101
Apr 29

These past days have been like a dream. Not making much sense, but still so real. The full-on hallucinations for Janet, the caregiving, trying to understand what she wants, what she needs, what is real, and what isn't. She starts to say something and stops a few words into her sentence, never finishing her thought. Natasha, Phillipe, David, Kenny, Nurse Cathy, Nurse Erik, Kaelan, Manda, Marlon, and I witnessed over the weekend the extreme confusion of Janet's hallucinations. Her body and brain are shutting down for many reasons, her organs and the low oxygen levels in her blood. Both nurses have said it's a matter of days now for Janet as her skin is "mottling" in a few places in addition to the other factors.

Marlon convinced me to try to get Janet outside again, so while Lois was here, we picked her up with all the bedding and carried her like she was on a stretcher to the cushion in the sun....
She was so happy to be outside. So, we all just sat in the sun for a couple of hours. It was hard to get her in and out, but we did it. She is still very confused about things, and she is still hard to understand.

I loved seeing her smile a lot yesterday. We started the day thinking that she had begun the "sleep coma," but just as Lois showed up about 11, she woke up ,and the shenanigans began again.
Erik came at 2 p.m., and Janet perked up for him as usual.
Her oxygen level was 85. He helped us with straightening out the bedding and tried to explain to Janet that she is really declining now and that the oxygen would help her feel more comfortable and that scheduled meds throughout the day would help.

She used the oxygen the rest of the day, and it went up to 87 before bed. But she still questions the meds every time....

I am going for a walk. It's 8 a.m. and a beautiful morning.

Day 102
Apr 30

Karen is arriving around 10:30 this morning. I've been wrong so many times, but I feel like Janet is going to pass today. She had a few hours of "death rattle" last night and then got very quiet for a few hours…. She was still breathing when I got up at 5:45 a.m., but had removed the oxygen at some point. I was burnt out from having the nurses here yesterday, so I went and met Kaelan at the Amber Side pub for dinner. I love him as a person, friend and son so much. Came home, sat with Marlon and Janet for a bit as she was up talking, using her phone, looking at a book. Gave her her meds and went to sleep at 9.

Day 103
May 2

Sitting by Janet's side in the bedroom after sleeping on the couch and a day trip to Vermont to go up Putney Mountain with Dagan to see the sunrise and the May Day Morris dancers. Then the Putney Diner, and then to visit with Elliot in Guilford, Vermont. I went with the blessing of Janet, Marlon, and Karen to take a day for myself, and accepted that if it was Janet's "time" while I was away, so be it. It was a beautiful day, sunny and warm. Elliot is putting his family dog down today, so there was a lot of sadness to share and stories to tell.

Got back at 7 p.m. Janet wanted to get into her chair, but when I came to the bedroom, she didn't have the strength to sit up, so she lay back down. I gave her medication, oxygen, and we all said goodnight about 9 p.m.

Another day.... She wakes up and, in a small voice, says, "It's time to get up," and wants to get into her chair. We agree, and then she closes her eyes and breathes. Nurse Erik is coming at 1 p.m.; Natalie is coming at 3; Lois is around all the time now, per my request, is staying at Kimberly's, and will probably be here around 11 or so. Janet spent the entire day in her chair in the living room. Karen and I used the stretcher method to get her there and back to the bedroom at 9:30 p.m.

Day 104
May 3

Beautiful sunny, warm day again this morning. Slept next to Janet, woke up, and held her hand for an hour. She is looking skeletal and peaceful this morning. Marlon is with their dad; Karen is out walking. It's nice and quiet, just the way I like it. Occasionally, Janet wakes up and looks at me, no expression on her face, just looks, turns her head, and goes back to closing her eyes and opening her mouth. Her breathing is soft and shallow. From time to time, I see her wrinkle her forehead like she is curious or frowning about something. She isn't in any pain or discomfort as far as we can tell. It seems that we have all done our best for her in all aspects of this end-of-life process, and I often wonder why she is still here with us. All I can think of is that her "being" isn't done being here yet in this physical manifestation. I don't see it as her "fighting" to hang on or that there is some unresolved issue needing to be dealt with, or a "goodbye" that needs to happen. Her body and mind just aren't totally done yet.... Somehow, her cells are still working to a certain degree even though it looks like her organs and body are not working anymore. The ultimate process of patience and letting go of what I expect and want and need. Just allowing Janet's process to be Janet's process, however long it takes.

It's been six weeks from yesterday since we brought her home for hospice, and at times has been the most difficult thing I have ever experienced.

Day 105
May 4

Today could be the day. Make sure to say at the memorial service, "I am sorry for our loss."

Yesterday afternoon, when everyone else got back from going into town for ice cream, Janet was in her chair and all of a sudden said, "I've got to pooop!" Even though she has an adult diaper on, she wanted to get on the toilet. So, we scrambled, readied the wheelchair, and very carefully and methodically managed to get her to the toilet. Karen and I had to balance her and support her weight. She didn't have the strength to hold her head up. After 15 minutes of moaning and groaning and almost throwing up, she managed to do two big normal poops!!! Then we stood her up, and after two attempts managed to wipe her butt, got her back in the wheelchair, and back into her chair. It was a small miracle and very intense for everyone.

Day 106
May 5

A Hunddred Last Breaths is the new name for the book. Kind of like the cat's nine lives. Janet keeps going, and we all take turns listening through the long pauses in her breathing. All night long, I kept waking up because of the long silence between extremely long and deep breaths. Poor Janet, her being just won't let go. She woke up at noon for an hour when the hospice brought a therapy dog for a visit. Good for everyone! I really thought she was going to pass in the middle of the night....
So I asked Lois to stay nearby. It's getting quieter in the house now because they all understand that Janet is getting closer....
Kimberly is here to "see" her and say a prayer. And of course, Nurse Erik shows up at exactly the same time.... Why is my heart racing? Kimberly said kind things, and I appreciate that.

Day 107
May 6

It's the silence between breaths that kept me awake last night, as well as the heavy sighs. Meds at 8:30 p.m., 12:45, 4:30, and 8:30 a.m. It feels like some sort of cosmic joke that Janet is still alive. I really feel terrible for her "hanging on" like this. Healthy Janet never would have wanted the end to be like this. I cried when I gave her meds at 4:30 because of her difficulty breathing and not being able to communicate with me what is really going on for her, and because of my inability to know if the meds are the right thing. There is no understanding why she is still alive. Her being isn't ready to stop being. So weak, so confused, so done… I'm not feeling like a very good caregiver.

Day 108
May 7

Marlon got a few words out of Janet yesterday morning; otherwise, she is unable to talk, barely able to lift her arms. And her eyes, when they are open, are rolled back in her head or staring at the ceiling. Her right eye is looking to the right, as her left eye is looking straight ahead. Nurse Cathy came with an apprentice yesterday as well as Nurse Claudia. They "fluffed" her, sponge bathed her, and changed her shirt and diaper, as well as her bedding and catheter bag. Then gave her meds at 2 p.m., so we are now continuing the meds every four hours: 6 p.m. me, 10 p.m. Marlon, 2 a.m. me, 6 a.m. this morning Karen. The nurses are coming every day now and think that Janet may or may not make it to the weekend. They say that she still might go through the "rag doll" stage, where she isn't able to move or do anything. Is my Janet still in that body? It's really hard to tell. The decline of her body and her mind makes it seem like she is just a shell, and Janet isn't there anymore. I hope she lets go today…. I love you, Janet Schuman, from high school.

**JANET PASSED AT 9:45 A.M.
ON MAY 8, 2025.**

Day 109
May 9

Janet passed away yesterday at 9:45 in the morning. I am so sad that it feels like my heart is actually physically broken. Twenty-four hours have passed, and the grief and sadness are so intense, I can barely breathe. I wasn't expecting how painful it feels. Apparently, you don't know how it feels until you are in it. She/we have been going through it for so long that I am going to miss taking care of her. Always being aware of her well-being and what she needs and wants at any particular time, day or night, all of a sudden isn't here anymore. Like someone turned out a light. Energy is there one moment and then it's not there anymore.... So quiet, so peaceful... I kissed her lips, and they were cold. Where did the warmth of those beautiful, loving lips go? Moments before, they were warm. How am I possibly going to get through this? I already feel so alone. Good night, Janet Schuman. I love you. Take me with you into your dreams. I wish I knew you are ok. Here I am left to feel all these hard feelings and emotional pain! Am I ever going to feel good again? Am I supposed to distract myself to not think about what she just went through these past weeks so I can bear to live? I am beyond sad.... I will have to sleep eventually.

Day 110
May 10

The sadness comes and goes in very intense waves, so I know there are times in between when my attention can be on other things that distract me from the sadness and pain. A pain I didn't know existed till now. Marlon, Karen, and Lois started to go through Janet's clothes yesterday while Kaelan and Manda were here, and we were all able to talk about other things and look at pictures, and tell stories of Janet that were happy. So, I have down waves of sadness and pain and up waves of distraction and productivity.... Cleaning, organizing, planning for the next moment, hour by hour. What to have to eat, what to do tomorrow.... I feel like it's not real.... I'm not going to see Janet ever again. I've been waiting for Janet to pass for so long and now...I just can't believe it.

Day 111
May 11

Kaelan, Manda, and Aja have been here for the past few days. Thank god! I needed them here for both Marlon and me. On and off emotions all weekend. Today is Mother's Day, and is especially hard for Marlon. I think a lot of people reached out to her today, and Leslie, Greg, and Gulia brought us all dinner and stayed to join us. Dagan arrived at 3:30, and it was a beautiful evening to eat outside. It was very sad to see Aja, Kaelan, and Manda go.

Tomorrow, Janet's body will be cremated. Kaelan, Dagan, and I will go and witness her body being put in the crematorium. It's going to be hard, but I feel I must for the finality of what we have been through with Janet's Journey. After Kaelan and Dagan leave tomorrow afternoon, it will get quiet.... Am I ready?

Day 112
May 13

Almost 11 p.m., and I am procrastinating on going to bed. Janet was cremated yesterday, and today I brought her home. It's all so very weird. Not sure what to do with myself. I've been taking care of Janet for so long. I miss her so very much. Kaelan and Dagan came with me to see Janet get put in the incinerator. I kissed her on her cold forehead and said, "Goodbye my dear Janet, take me with you." I sobbed when I got back in my car.

I could sob right now if I think of all the things Janet went through and all her suffering I witnessed. I started Therapy with Debbie from Ann's Place today. I think we are a good fit and will continue each week. I gave a rundown of the past five-and-a-half years and some of what Janet and I endured, and now everything that comes with the death of my beloved Janet. I have to sleep now.

Day 113
May 14

Am I ready to write about the last 48 hours of Janet's life experience? The trauma I have around the meds and the time of the meds and the couple of terrifying screams of pain....

Day 114
May 15

Went to bed last night so sad and so quiet…. Woke up sobbing
into my coffee…oh, the pain!!! Of my broken heart. Letting it
come and letting it go. I miss Janet so much! Yesterday, Marlon
and I went to see Dana at the yoga studio for an hour. That was
hard. I gave Dana her Christmas gifts from Janet that never got
wrapped because she was too sick, and I met Jenny, whom I have
heard a lot about. Giovanna sent us dinner…I don't remember
what else. Today, deep sadness and putzing around. Suzy brought
us lunch. I think we were the first ones she has talked to about
losing a dear friend. I sobbed after she left, curled up on the
bed…then took another bath and kept putzing around. Made a
shrine on the bookshelf with Janet's ashes, Mom and Dad's ashes,
and some pictures of beautiful Janet and Amy.

Day 115
May 16

Janet's pain and suffering were not my pain and suffering. My trauma is and was watching her pain and suffering. Her choices and how those choices affected me and our relationship. She apologized to me many times over the past five-and-a-half years, saying, "This isn't what you signed up for." But actually, when you are deeply in love with someone, it is what you "sign up for. My deep love is what made it possible to take care of her in the best way I could. I wanted her to have comfort and relief always, and it hurt me so much to watch her go through surgery after surgery, chemo after chemo...and ultimately her decline. Her pain, her choices, her suffering, her fear...her struggle. These things were hers...not mine.

People say to me, "You've been through a lot." Yes, I have, but at the same time, it was all driven by my deep love for Janet. I miss her so much! I miss what we had before cancer, and I miss taking care of her during cancer. It was a lot and really fuckin hard....
It's just the way it was.

Day 116
May 18

I drove to Essex to stay with Ken and Lois for the weekend.

Because I pretty much only went there with Janet over the past 16 years, it was pretty hard when I first got here. I lay on Janet's side of the bed where we usually slept, and wept.... Feelings about the last time Janet was here at Christmas, when she could barely move and talk, curled up on the sofa, listening to the activity going on around her as people made small talk. While there, I decided to re-read all my journal entries of the past six months. I feel that I would like to turn them into a book. I wasn't sure before, but now I think I have to. Then I went for a long walk in the local cemetery and into town for ice cream at Sweet Peas and to sit on a bench at the Connecticut River Museum overlooking the Connecticut River. It was a beautiful day and a good walk that I had done many times over the years with Janet. When I got back to the house, I started painting Janet's memorial rocks that I will give away at Janet's celebration on July 10. My goal is to paint 150 for people to take and put in their gardens or flower pots. It's a beautiful sunny day here today and I feel... ok. Ok is better than sad, so I'll take it. I know the sad can and will come back at any moment. I think reading through the trauma has helped me.

Day 117
May 19

Back home, opened the shades this morning to let in the light. I'm glad I went to Essex. It felt right. I started making the memorial stones for Janet's celebration, and I have painted 30 so far. Looking at her birth date and death dates on the stones, 3/29/65 - 5/8/25, is weird—an end date of being in her body. It's just so weird that she isn't here next to me, breathing in bed, to hold my hand or say hi when I walk in the door. The partnership of life is a sharing of life, sharing of the wonders and exciting stuff, as well as the mundane—the teeth brushing, the gaining and losing weight, the sitting with morning coffees. The news of someone getting married or a friend's child graduating from college.... The sharing of life. That is what I am missing.

Day 118
May 20

I found some old Janet notebooks with details of her skydiving days, and looked at some pictures of me and Janet from 15 years ago in NYC. I really miss those days of our relationship when we were both physically beautiful, healthy, and in love.
I was infatuated with being in love with Janet! Her smallness, her style, her long hair, her beautiful eyes and lips, and our lovemaking! I loved our dreams back then of being in love into our old age, and we both pictured ourselves holding hands into our 80s and being there for each other all the way to the end, which I know I was for her.... Just 25 years earlier than expected.

Twelve days gone, I miss you so much! I'll be sure to take you into my dreams, dear sweet Janet.

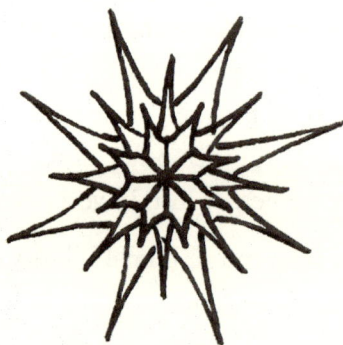

EPILOGUE

The numbers game. I still count the days and weeks and am now into months. Although I am still journaling every day and don't feel like I need to include any of the past few weeks, I do want to share some thoughts about what I have written, along with some things that will hopefully fill in some gaps and explain more of what I felt during different parts of this journey.

Christmas

Leading up to Christmas Day was particularly rough. Aunts, uncles, and cousins were all getting together at Janet's mom's house, an hour and a half away. Janet was so ill leading up to it that she didn't want to go. I think she felt that she didn't have the energy to socialize even with family, and she definitely didn't want to put on a "face" we so often do at holidays. She didn't want to have to explain what or how she was feeling, and at the same time didn't want me or Marlon to miss out on Christmas dinner. She didn't want to miss out either, but she could barely move. I refused to go without her, and I was ok with staying at home with her, even though Kaelan and Manda were going to be there from Brooklyn just for dinner. Ultimately, I think that is why she decided to push herself to go.

When we arrived at Janet's mom's, I helped her to the sofa in the living room, where she curled up into a ball with her eyes closed. She wasn't sleeping; she just wanted to be a part of the family as everyone else conversed and ate their cheese and crackers. Everyone seemed to respect this and took turns sitting with her or holding her hand. I would occasionally check on her with a kiss on the head and ask her if she wanted to move into the bedroom. It was the last family gathering with Janet, and it seemed everyone knew it was going to be.

Hope Lodge

The days leading up to the proton radiation in January were another time where I was in a sort of survival mode. Janet was declining so fast. Her skin was changing to an olive color, and the whites of her eyes were becoming a neon yellow because her liver was not processing anything properly. She was suffering so much with the tumor pressing against her bile ducts and digestive system that all I could focus on was getting her to the treatment and Hope Lodge. Karen flew into NYC to take over the logistics of getting Janet back and forth from Midtown to Harlem each day. All we were hoping for was some relief for her from the pressure and problems the tumor was causing, which it did. By the time Karen came and took over, I was completely burnt out, unable to put pencil to paper to write. I got home and slept, showered, cleaned, walked, slept some more, went to the movies, ate shitty food…and paced around the empty house for days. At this point, I almost had a breakdown, so I asked Lena and Michael to fly up from Florida to help me out. I think I was in denial and scared about what the future would look like without Janet in my life.

The Mystery

Right after Janet passed away and up until a month after, I struggled with the unknowingness of what happened to Janet's being, her essence, the Janet soul that I always felt so connected to. You can say I was distraught at times; yes, the grief was huge, but I so badly needed to know that she was at peace. Before she left her body, I had always believed a person's essence or being would go to a place of all knowingness, a oneness with all things, to become part of the vast god source, some might call that heaven. I thought I would be able to feel her go to such a place after she left her body. But I felt nothing around my connection with her, which made me sad beyond belief. As time has passed, I have meditated on these feelings and have spoken about this with many friends and family. I am now at the point where I am open to any signs that I may receive from the different realms where Janet's essence may be, especially in nature and other types of "coincidences" that have no explanation and feel like they could be guided by Janet, including dreams. There have been many.

The Celebration

On July 10, we celebrated Janet's beautiful life. As she wished, at the Yoga Loft, with the music playlist she wanted, with the food she wanted, provided by the Tavern. Over 200 people showed up. The celebration was amazingly beautiful in every way—the flowers, the food, the pictures, the music, the hugging, and the love, which was palpable in the room. It was a huge milestone for me. Leading up to it, I was a nervous wreck at times, after all, I had been thinking about this day for quite a while. The kind of nervousness you experience when you are putting on a party and don't know if people are going to come, or you don't know if the food is going to be good. Even though I had practiced what I was going to say a few times, I was still nervous...until I showed up and the pre-party jitters disappeared. There were already people arriving to help assemble the flowers, the pictures, and the tables for the rocks. People started hugging me, and kept hugging me. I'd turn around to see someone else who was part of Janet's life, from her childhood to the present. They all wanted to hug me. With every hug, the tears kept flowing. It felt like the tears were being squeezed out of me, which felt good. It can be a scary and very vulnerable place to be. To stand up in front of 200 people with a microphone, with everyone's eyes on you and ears intent on hearing what you have to say about someone that they loved. I didn't stick to the script exactly but communicated what I wanted to convey along with a Cat Stevens song that I sang without accompaniment.... I had never done anything like that before. The support I am still receiving from people near and far keeps me buoyed every day. When I look back, I feel it really was everything that she and I hoped it would be.

Intimacy

As you can see, this is a very intimate and personal sharing of what I was going through, emotionally, physically, and spiritually as Janet was transitioning, and still am. Not only the intimacy of sharing this story. Perhaps the word "intimacy" should be explored and clarified so that it is not mistaken or misinterpreted. Yes, of course, there is the part of the many years of lack of sexual sharing, but there is the changing of an intimate relationship to be considered. The intimate feelings. Sadness, love, tenderness, anger and resentment, compassion, sympathy, upset, acceptance, as well as the remembering of shared joyful memories.... And of course, grief. Grief, after the first few weeks. Grief comes in waves for me, and I think it does for everyone who lives through a loss. Grief to me is also part of the intimacy of the relationship I have with Janet.

The Dream

Today I woke up feeling ok, with a sense of calm after having Janet come to me in a dream. Her face filled my vision; there was an expression on her beautiful Janet face to say that everything is alright. Not contentment, not concern, but almost an expression that wasn't a human perception. It was the first time she came through clearly, taking up the full vision of my mind's eye, and as beautiful as ever. I woke up, and after a couple hours of taking care of myself, the grief hit hard. I still can't believe she is not physically here with me. I still have waves of grief and disbelief. I have been told that this will continue, with the waves getting less frequent and less intense… and so, I Accept…with Compassion…and Love.

Why Write the Book?

My brother-in-law asked me, "Why did you write this book, and what is your intention in sharing it?" Now that I can read it, I feel that I can step back and notice that I was given a gift, not only to support Janet with the end of her life, but to witness. Not only her struggles, but my own. Yes, I wrote this book for myself, to help me process the loss of my beloved. But I also wrote this book to share my experience with my friends and family, as well as anyone who has gone through or is going through some sort of loss and is experiencing grief. I have found solace in knowing that I am not alone with the feelings I have, particularly over the last seven months of Janet's life and the past few months since she passed away.

I hope that if you are reading this and any of it resonates with you—the love, the devotion, the pain, the struggle, the difficult logistics of taking care of someone with a terminal illness, the feelings of wanting to escape from it all—I hope you feel some sort of relief that you are not the only one going through it. I hope you understand that there is help available. If the help isn't coming to you automatically, you may have to reach out to others. Family, friends, extended family, support groups, and organizations of all kinds are there ready and willing to help you…to help you with logistics, food, medicines, therapy, time away, and especially grief. Please know that you are not alone.

I WEEP FOR THE TREE

Stopped, dead in my tracks

As I look up and see

That my dear friend has fallen

Shocked in disbelief as I stare

I begin to weep for the tree

I slowly start walking and then stop

Unable to move closer

To be with this being I have hugged many times

That now lies on the ground with a fractured body

In its resting place after years of preparation... for the fall

Rotting, home to many creatures

Insects, squirrels, birds, mushrooms, and moss

Patiently waiting for the moment when gravity takes its toll

I weep uncontrollably for the tree

Surprised by the emotion washing over me.. I allow it to come

*I touch the tree and remember all the conversations I had as I
        slowed my pace to recognize its grace*

How many times did I say to her... "It's ok to let go"?

How many times did I think "This could be the day"?

Always expecting and knowing the end is near

I weep for the tree

A long life it had, weathering the seasons that nature had to offer

*The gentle breezes, the stiff freezing cold of winter, and
        the winds... oh the winds... that represent the change
        of the seasons and new things to come.*

To see and feel the tree lying there with its rotten insides and
pulpy flesh spread about the forest

Fallen with such a dead weight force against the ground

I wonder about the sound… that is now so silent and still

I weep for the tree… or do I weep for me?

Helpful Resources

www.griefshare.org/
Grief Share is a grief recovery support group where you can find help and healing for the hurt of losing a loved one.

988 Suicide and crisis lifeline.
A national network available 24/7 via call, text, or chat, offering support for individuals experiencing mental health crises.

www.nami.org
NAMI Connection Recovery Support Group: A free, peer-led support group for adults experiencing mental health conditions.

Crisis Text Hotline
Offers text-based support by texting HELLO to 741741.

The American Cancer Society:
https://www.cancer.org/support-programs-and-services.html

Connect with others in support groups for cancer patients, loved ones, and people who have lost a loved one, led by oncology social workers at:
www.cancercare.org

Final Gifts: Understanding the Special Awareness, Needs and Communications of the Dying
by Maggie Callanan and Patricia Kelly

Matthew and Janet
May 2024

Matthew Broad is a teacher of expressing feelings through the arts of drumming and painting mandalas. An avid journal keeper, he has learned to love life after going through and witnessing the death process of his beloved partner.

For information regarding
signings and speaking engagements,
please contact Matthew at:

www.ahundredlastbreaths@gmail.com

www.ingramcontent.com/pod-product-compliance
Lightning Source LLC
Chambersburg PA
CBHW030527100426
42813CB00001B/176